Elders and Deacons and Saints, Oh My!

Defining Biblical Roles, Structure and Organization for a Team Ministry that Achieves the Fivefold Purpose of the Church

"To my fellow ***elders*** *I make this request of you: Be like* ***shepherds*** *as you guide the flock of God under your care – serving as their* ***overseers****; not because you have to, but because you desire to please God. Do not serve for the purpose of getting something out of it, but rather from an eagerness to minister to others; do not be bossy - lording your position over those trusted to your care by God, instead serve as an example to them."*

1 Peter 5:1-3
(Author's Translation)

James Kirkland

CrossBooks™
A Division of LifeWay
1663 Liberty Drive
Bloomington, IN 47403
www.crossbooks.com
Phone: 1-866-879-0502

First published by CrossBooks 4/19/2011

ISBN: 978-1-6150-7823-3 (sc)
ISBN: 978-1-6150-7824-0 (dj)

Library of Congress Control Number: 2011926607

Printed in the United States of America

This book is printed on acid-free paper.

To my wife Virginia

You are the proof I needed to know that God really does love me! You are to me the wife described in Proverbs 31:10-31. Thank you for spending your life with me. I love you.

Table of Contents

PREFACE

8:30 A.M. More new people here again! Six months after starting this service, two hundred people come to worship, a fourfold increase. Soon, we would buy a facility for worship. God's work amazed me on that day, and, looking back, it still does.

It's Thursday night, time to start the next class teaching people how to study the bible for themselves. I am amazed at the hunger these people have for the Word of God and the way in which it is changing their lives. We started with just 15 people the first time the class was offered. A little over year later and nearly 300 people have become engaged in study, some have been saved and all have developed a healthy desire for His Word.

This snapshot brings together the dream that underlies this book. In this dream, each church has leadership based on Scripture, a sense of followship among the congregation, and teamwork that unites and empowers all to pursue their calling.

Unfortunately, the reality is that the church today has a crisis of leadership. Despite the many books written on leadership, both by Christians and non-Christians, many elders, pastors, deacons and saints still struggle to understand their role as Scripture lays it out, let alone function together in loving relationships that appear different from the surrounding culture. This book seeks to overturn misunderstanding and clarify the Scriptural plan, and it is my fervent desire that it helps everyone to better understand the role of the leader and the followers; to help you move away from "Church, Inc." and learn to love the development of people for Christ.

This book emerges out of my own journey as I experienced this crisis of leadership. As a new Christian, I continued to walk, for the most part, as I had before my conversion. Only a number of years later did my heart become transformed as well as my head. I thank God for a teaching elder who provided the mentoring and encouragement I needed to change how I lived for Christ. The eighteen inches from the head to the heart can be a tremendously long journey! Once that transformation took place, God worked mightily to show me His heart for the church by providing the vision that became, *Elders and Deacons and Saints, Oh My.*

As a result, I left behind my business career as a financial planner, attended seminary, and began a new career as a pastor. Even as I pursued this vocational shift, I became a leader in the church as an elder. I also founded a ministry to assist churches as they sought to fulfill God's purposes for the church, specifically by teaching people how to read the Bible for themselves and developing a process to help believers become mature disciples. Drawing heavily on my experience as a manager, team builder and planner combined with knowledge of Scripture I provided assistance to help churches write clear mission and vision statements designed to achieve the mission given by Christ Himself. In that role, I have seen the crisis of leadership firsthand, and I have seen too many churches experience disunity and fracture, stress and high turnover.

I have conducted significant research these past several years, observing a variety of Evangelical Churches to identify what is working and what is not. My research has allowed first hand observation of Baptist, Charismatic, Presbyterian, Lutheran, Evangelical Free and Non Denominational churches as well as those who follow the Purpose Driven or Willow Creek models. A few of these can be described as very successful at accomplishing the mission of both making disciples and reaching the lost. Most of them have been failing. I have observed in every case the failure being caused by a crisis of leadership.

At the heart of this crisis is a leadership that fails to shepherd and care for their people while also leading them into a life of genuine discipleship as they work together to reach the lost. Some churches have become so focused on the numbers that growing the church has replaced the need to provide encouragement and care to those who believe and serve. I have recently seen many people become burned out in a church that puts an unreasonable expectation on "production" and fails to provide their own members and staff with what I like to call "RAP" – Recognition, Appreciation, and Praise. The word "ruthless" is more applicable to this high turnover church than "encourager" which should be the expectation of every church.

Yet many other churches have become so focused on themselves that they fail to reach the lost at all. The evangelical church in America has earned a reputation, and much of it is not good. In his book by the same name, Ravi Zacharias posed the question, "Has Christianity Failed You?" Sadly, for many people the answer is a resounding "yes."

What if, instead of fracture and hurt, more churches experienced teamwork and empowerment? What if more churches could learn to serve together in genuine loving relationships that really help people grow in their knowledge of God's Word and mature in their faith while also reaching the lost? In God's plan, pastors, elders, deacons and saints work together to fulfill God's purpose, each having their own role. Most of you who pick up this book have accepted Jesus Christ. You are, in truth, "saints" in the church of Jesus Christ. Many of you have matured in the faith and have been called to be elders or deacons or other leaders.

Some of you are wrestling with the meaning of that calling and want to understand what Scripture says about your role and your task. Others are being asked to identify those serving among you who could serve as an elder and you wonder what the Scriptural requirements are for the position. It is my dream that this book will help you answer those questions. For those of you who do not yet know Jesus as Lord and Savior, get to know Him. Read and study the Scripture. Pray. Ask for a mature believer or an elder or pastor to teach you. Then find someone to walk alongside you as you pursue your calling as a disciple of Jesus. And then you go, and make disciples too.

It is my fervent desire that this book will help forward your journey as you seek to follow Scripture, to move your church forward in the fivefold purpose that God has given us. May God speed you and your church on the way to achieving what Christ wants us to achieve so that, in the end, we may hear Him say, "Well done!"

CHAPTER I

"For God is not a God of disorder but of peace. As in all the congregations of the saints"

- 1 Cor 14:33[1]

Introduction

Why do we need another book about elders and church government?

Candidly, it is because the church is failing in many ways to achieve the mission Christ gave us. This failure is especially true in a culture in which truth has become subjective at best. We hardly even know what the mission is anymore. An inability to articulate our faith, to explain why we believe what we believe, and to explain Scripture to a friend or neighbor has become normal. There are many churches today that appear successful as measured by the number of people who attend and the size of their facility but consider the depth of the relationships they have with each other and wonder, "How does this model loving relationships or demonstrate caring service?" There is a reason why many churches fail to connect believers to a life of growing maturity, who burn out their employees and servants with excessive expectations of artificial growth that results in as many people going out the back door as are coming in the front door. And, there is a reason why many other churches fail to grow at all.

Disciple making has fallen on hard times in our country. As a result, evangelical Christians will either be equipped and successful or hamstrung and ineffective at the leadership level. It is here that loving servant leadership will be demonstrated or not. Leaders who serve and love and equip those people who work and volunteer will create an environment that encourages the "saints" to connect with people and make disciples and it is in this that the church of Jesus Christ will achieve its mission. To "elder" or not to "elder," that is the question. In recent years there has been a great deal of debate, even arguments, over the correct form of government within Christianity.

Any organization in pursuit of a vision requires good working relationships in order to be successful. Effective teamwork, organization, shared vision and obedience to leadership can only happen when the process is managed well and is surrounded by a genuine love of people. Scripture is quite clear about the form of government expected of the body. This system of government provides both the organization and the management style needed for the New Testament church to achieve its purpose. The mission, the system, and the expected results are all laid out in God's Word. While ample room for flexibility and variety exists within God's plan, the general format of His government is clearly laid out in His Word. So then, why are there such differing opinions and controversies over church government? The short answer is found in a single word: "Obedience." Or more aptly stated: "It is the lack thereof."

The Bible pictures a New Testament church being led by servant leaders known generally as elders. They are also called overseers, bishops, pastors, or shepherds. They are expected to lead but also to work in cooperation with their flock. To some degree, responsibility and authority are shared in a congregational form of government. A balance exists between oversight and obedience, leading and teaching, and serving and cooperation. As believers mature and as the need arises, additional elders, deacons and ministry leaders are selected, preferably from among the spiritually mature and obedient members of the congregation, and appointed to serve by their elders.

Extremes of "rule" should be avoided at either end of the spectrum. God admonishes elders not to "Lord it over" their flock, but rather to be "servant leaders." He never intended for decision making to be vested in voting by all members, but rather for everyone to model obedience. Trusting, obedient, and cooperative relationships are the expectation of Scripture.

The existence of order within God's kingdom is evident throughout Scripture and should be illustrated by our love for and service to one another. The New Testament church certainly is expected to have some form of organization that leads toward continuity and order. In every sphere, there can be no peace or prosperity without rule according to God, for He is not the Author of confusion but of peace.[2] For this purpose, Scripture has affirmed a special office of authority through which the government of the church is to be organized and managed: the office of elder.

Those who oppose this concept generally misunderstand the use of the word as it appears in both the Old and New Testaments. Sloppy word studies have led some to believe the word simply means older person and has nothing to do with an office of authority: this is simply not so. As is the case with any word, it can and often does take on different meanings. Context is the most basic and important thing to remember in Bible study. I can say "I love my wife" and "I love pizza." "Love" is the same word with a different meaning in each sentence. What if I were to use a word that is not even a word like "Bub?" I can say, "Please turn on the light bub" or "Hey, bub, please turn on the light." We can only understand what a word means from its relationship with the other words in a sentence, its "context." So it is with elder, overseer, pastor, and deacon. Mistakes in word meaning are often made when people forget how to read a book, or may not have accumulated the knowledge necessary to read a book effectively in the first place.[3] The Bible is literature. It follows basic rules of grammar, and context is king when it comes to studying it.

I will demonstrate that in many passages, the Bible is referring to one and the same person when it uses the terms "elder or presbyter," "overseer or bishop," and "pastor or shepherd." The office of *elder* is to be occupied by an *overseer* who acts like a *shepherd* and is responsible for leading the flock while fulfilling the duties of managing God's household. The elder is a leader and an ambassador charged with the job of governing as a manager or steward. In a variety of New Testament passages, these terms are used interchangeably to describe the same person. Scripture places so much emphasis on the importance of the "elder" in managing the affairs of God that a single word is apparently not sufficient by itself to describe who and what the elder is and does. A clear understanding of this special function of church government can only come from considering the meaning of the words as they appear in context of the original languages. Studying the variety of words in context will make it possible to knit together a working definition based on the collective meaning of the terms applied to the elder. The appendix will provide you with a fairly exhaustive word study of the terms for these leaders, as well as for deacons. It includes my conclusions, and I encourage you to take the time to study it.

It is not possible for anyone to lead or govern a people who refuse to follow. A leader, by definition, needs followers. New Testament elders are called to be servant leaders who guide the congregation, using Scripture and sound doctrine as the authority for their direction, set a personal example for a congregation to follow, and equip them for works of service. The reason for having a proper relationship between elders and the congregation is to achieve the fivefold purpose Christ gave to the church as found in Matthew 22:37-40 and Matthew 28:19, which I will explain more fully in the next section.

In accomplishing the mission Scripture describes a fellowship of loving people who, being directed by the Holy Spirit, work in cooperation with and submission to their leaders. Elders have the responsibility to lead and congregations are expected to follow and obey them (Heb 13:17). Servant leadership, sound teaching, and caring relationships are necessary ingredients. It becomes important to understand God's expectation and requirements of elders, who will ultimately be held accountable for the way in which they fulfill their duties. We will explore this further in the coming chapters. Before that, we will consider the fivefold purpose, the mission given by Christ and the reason why He gave it. The system of government provided in Scripture is for the purpose of achieving His plan and purpose. To understand His plan, we should start with a basic understanding of sin and an understanding of why the mission is vitally important.

Understanding the Mission and the Need for an Effective Organization

The mission was given because of the need for salvation. People need to hear the good news of how Christ solved the problem of sin. First, we must answer the question: what is sin? It might be tempting to skip over this section because it may be a review of the basics: a statement of what you may already know. But understanding sin and our mission is important if we are to see the need to follow clear Biblical instruction for government. The organizational model provided in Scripture is for the purpose of addressing sin and accomplishing the mission statement given by Christ in two statements known as "The Great Commandment" and "The Great Commission." Beginning with a review of what may seem obvious will ensure that we are working with the same starting point when we go on to define organization, relationships, and leadership roles.

Understanding "sin" is not particularly difficult. When my faith was new, I attended a party with numerous members of the local "New Age" type church and participated in a religious discussion. It did not take long before the conversation turned to Jesus and the concept of sin. These folks deny that Jesus is God and do not believe He died for the forgiveness of our sin. Being a new believer and not well versed in the Bible, I was soon in over my head. In responding to my assertion that all have sinned and need Jesus to be saved, one of their leaders asked a question in a very challenging way, saying, "Do you honestly believe that a precious little newborn baby is born in sin?" The hum of conversation in the room stopped and you could have heard a pin drop as folks waited for the response from the only born again believer at the party. What a failure I was. Shocked by the gravity of the question, I could not answer it, and my faith was rocked for weeks to come—that is, until I came to an understanding of what sin is and why we need a Savior. I thank God for a teaching elder who was able to give me proper *instruction* in order to *equip* me for future encounters while *showing* me how to be a disciple!

In the NIV Bible the word sin appears 917 times in one variation or another (sin, sinner, sinned, sins, etc). The Old Testament had numerous words all translated "sin" but having various meanings like "wicked, guilty, bad, criminal, weak, etc." The Hebrew חַטָּאת (pronounced chattath) conveys the same general meaning as we find in the New Testament, "missing the road or mark."[4] It is generally used to convey a sin or transgression against God.

In the New Testament "sin" is most often translated from the Greek word ἁμαρτία (pronounced hamartia) and conveys the primary meaning of "missing the mark."[5] It is a very comprehensive term for moral deficiency as represented by our separation or distance from God. We may find a correlation, from a teaching or preaching perspective, to a measure of distance as found in ancient archery. By way of illustration, archers would set up targets and practice with bow and arrow. They would measure the distance between their arrow and the bullseye to see how far they missed the mark. The distance between them is a mathematical measurement that could be referred to as "sin." Though the word is not directly tied to archery in ancient texts, it is illustrative of how "sin" impacts our relationship with God. It provides a picture of our distance, or separation, from God. Therefore, sin can be defined simply as "the distance between where God is and where I am." Anything that captures our attention and occupies our thoughts so that our focus is not on God and His plan for our life is sin. When we focus on ourselves or our own needs with a "me first" attitude that excludes God, we sin.

We find the account of the fall of man in Genesis 3. God had told Adam and Eve they could "eat" or take into themselves anything from the garden except for one thing, *"but you must not eat from the tree of the knowledge of good and evil, for when you eat of it you will surely die."* (Genesis 2:17). The enemy, Satan the serpent, confused Eve and convinced her that they could be equal to God. In his conversation with Eve he told her a lie that set up a way of thinking that led to separation from God: *"You will not surely die, the serpent said to the woman. For God knows that when you eat of it your eyes will be opened, and you will be like God, knowing good and evil."* (Genesis 3:4-5).

It is pretty simple to grasp the significance of this event. Who knows everything? Here is a hint; it's not you or me. Only God knows everything. Only God is able to understand what is good or evil, right or wrong. Apart from God it is not possible for man to know the difference; this has been proven over and over throughout history. A dear friend of mine likes to say, "If everyone is god, what happens when two gods are in a room and they disagree?" The idea that it is possible to be equal to God is the ultimate lie of Satan that caused us to become separated from God. Sin caused a fracture that put distance between God and us. It was the dawning of a movement teaching everyone, "You have the capacity to be God or His equal, so you do not need God." It teaches us to be selfish rather than selfless: to be self focused rather than God focused. It set us on a path that has led to humanistic thought and postmodern relativism. My friends, there is nothing new about New Age thought. It is the original sin.

This event brought sin to us and caused man to fall away from his eternal personal relationship and walk with God. When man decided it was good to call his own shots, to make his own decisions about what is right or wrong, he became separated from God saying, "I can do it myself." Instead of daily focusing on God and seeking Him for direction, we ourselves became the focus and the authority. We became "selfish," meaning "focused on our wants and desires at the exclusion of God and His people." The distance between us and God is called "sin." We sin against Him in a variety of ways, but mostly in our lack of love for Him and in our failure to apply worth to Him. By the way, the word "worship" actually means "worth-ship," placing God as most valuable over everything including ourselves (especially ourselves).

When God called Adam into account for his actions, Adam's response is compelling. I have heard it said that Adam's response to God was to blame Eve, and this began the so called "blame game" that infected mankind. I think we need to put the emphasis on a different word. Scripture tells us that Adam replied to God, saying, *"The woman you put here with me - she gave me some fruit from the tree, and I ate."* (Genesis 3:12). Try reading this verse while placing the emphasis on the word "you" instead of the word "woman." It makes a big difference. Sin caused man to think he knows better than God. Adam blamed God Himself for the problem of sin. How arrogant is that?

Ever since the fall, man has been desperately trying to figure out a way to enter the perfect paradise God created. Hell is a real place and we have an intuitive desire to avoid going there. We make our best efforts to be good people, to live good lives in the hope of justifying ourselves. We try to be good enough or do enough good deeds to earn our way back home, as if there was some kind of heavenly score card or something. We try to live a life perfectly, like an arrow that hits the bullseye. But we cannot, because sin is like a magnet surrounding the target, causing every shot to pull the arrow away from the bullseye.

The Bible illustrates the difference between a life lived our way and a life lived according to His Spirit. A life lived according to the "sinful nature" produces very different results from a life lived according to the "Spirit" of God (Galatians 5:16-25). Read through this passage and ask yourself, "Which camp do I want to be in?" A follower of Christ should demonstrate a gradual diminishing of the fruit produced by the sinful nature and a gradual increase in fruit produced by the Spirit of God in us. Make note that the word "Spirit" is capitalized in scripture. A small "s" would mean our spirit. The capital "S" means God's Spirit, the Holy Spirit, our Helper.

> *"So I say, live by the Spirit, and you will not gratify the desires of the sinful nature. For the sinful nature desires what is contrary to the Spirit, and the Spirit what is contrary to the sinful nature. They are in conflict with each other, so that you do not do what you want. But if you are led by the Spirit, you are not under law. The acts of the sinful*

> *nature are obvious: sexual immorality, impurity and debauchery; idolatry and witchcraft; hatred, discord, jealousy, fits of rage, selfish ambition, dissensions, factions and envy; drunkenness, orgies, and the like. I warn you, as I did before, that those who live like this will not inherit the kingdom of God. But the fruit of the Spirit is love, joy, peace, patience, kindness, goodness, faithfulness, gentleness and self-control. Against such things there is no law. Those who belong to Christ Jesus have crucified the sinful nature with its passions and desires. Since we live by the Spirit, let us keep in step with the Spirit (Galatians 5:16-25).*

When I read this passage I am struck by the fact that God links together the concepts of "idolatry and witchcraft." An idol is pretty much anything we want out of our self focus. It could be money and possessions or anything else we want in our sin apart from God. These selfish desires come from a sinful nature that separated us from Him in the first place. And what is witchcraft if not the casting spells for the express purpose of getting something you want? Many a prayer is lifted up to God for the express purpose of getting what we want, and when we don't get it we become angry with God just like Adam did way back then. Prayers that are completely self focused are just a form of spell casting and the scripture calls this "witchcraft."

When it comes to sin, no matter how good a shot we become or how hard we try, we will never hit the bullseye unless God does the aiming. Yes, even a precious newborn baby is born with this problem. A problem caused by a "me first" attitude, no matter how innocent it may appear. A price must be paid for sin: judgment has to be made. Just to be clear, I am not saying a child is excluded from heaven. That is another subject entirely, but I do believe there comes a time when everyone reaches an age where a decision must be made. In Christ we can escape the judgment we deserve for we are no longer under condemnation of the law (Galatians 5:18). Choose salvation, not justice! Where are you in this decision?

Life is full of consequences that serve as examples of justice. Our actions have repercussions. Sometimes our actions bring judgment and ramifications that are very difficult to deal with. The judgment for sin results in eternal separation from God. If we choose to go our own way, be our own god and find ourselves still in this state of rebellion when we die, we spend eternity in a place we will not want to be: a place where God allows us the freedom to live without Him. This is described as a place of torment. In essence, this is the Hebrew concept of the place called hell. It is our choice to go there, not God's, and He will not force our arrow to the bullseye against our will. What a wonder that God created us with free will, and how devastating too. But a robot cannot love its creator; it can only do what it was programmed to do. Satan wanted to be elevated above God. It led to his fall from heaven. Mankind decided he did not need God. It led to eternal separation from God. We are responsible for bringing sin into the world, not God. It was our choice to do so, and it remains our choice to love and obey Him or reject Him in favor of our own selfishness. In Christ we have the freedom to choose between receiving the gift of forgiveness or getting the justice we deserve.

It is wonderful good news to know that God could not bear the thought of spending eternity without us. So, He devised a plan to rescue us Himself. He would provide a way to bridge the gap and remove the obstacle of sin by covering it Himself. For that reason, the evangelical church loves to recite from the Gospel of John:

> *"For God so loved the world that he gave his one and only Son, that whoever believes in him shall not perish but have eternal life. For God did not send his Son into the world to condemn the world, but to save the world through him. Whoever believes in him is not condemned, but whoever does not believe stands condemned already because he has not believed in the name of God's one and only Son.* (John 3:16-18)

Whatever our sin or sinful desire is, it puts all of us in a spiritual prison cell of our own choosing. We were born with it. Yet, Jesus has unlocked the door! All you have to do is open it and come out and follow Him. But He will not force you to do so. You are free to remain separated from Him, forever. How sad. But it does not have to be that way. The word "gospel" comes from the Greek word, εὐαγγέλιον (pronounced euangelion). Guess what it means: *The Good News!* The Lord expects us to spread this Good News in order to achieve the mission of helping people get out of that prison cell while showing them what life with God can be like and how to live a full life in Christ. To preach the gospel is the same thing as to proclaim the good news. We are to be His hands and feet among a people who are perishing apart from Him, a people who are in desperate need of a personal relationship with the Savior. Jesus gave us a purpose, a mission statement, and a system of organization to help us accomplish that purpose. But just what is the mission?

The Fivefold Purpose of the Church

The fivefold purpose of the church describes the mission. We find it in the words of Jesus as found in Matthew 22:37-40 and Matthew 28:18-20.

Our mission statement as a church representing Jesus Christ is summarized in two of his teachings, which can be developed into five specific things He expects us to accomplish.

They are:

1. Love God (with all you've got!)
2. Love others
3. Evangelism
4. Identification
5. Discipleship

Jesus provided the first two purposes of the church when he explained the greatest commandment. A teacher of the law had asked Him, "What is the greatest commandment?" Jesus answered, *"'Love the Lord your God with all your heart and with all your soul and with all your mind.' This is the first and greatest commandment. And the second is like it: 'Love your neighbor as yourself.' All the Law and the Prophets hang on these two commandments"* (Matthew 22:37-40). From this passage we can identify the first two of the five purposes of the church:

Love God

Jesus establishes the importance of a vertical relationship with Him. This relationship has to exist before we can have genuine loving relationships with each other, the horizontal relationships. Have you ever thought about all those Old Testament sacrifices and rituals? They were many and frequent and had the main purpose of keeping His people from forgetting Him: to help them focus not on themselves, but God. Imagine a daily routine for living that places our relationship with God first in everything, every day for our entire lives. In remembering God and His prior acts of love and faithfulness, an environment was created in daily living that was intended to be always focused on God. It should be the same for a follower of Jesus today. Our focus should be on God, not because of rules and rituals to follow but because He has changed and entered our hearts. The vertical relationship with Him comes before we can enjoy loving relationships with each other. The first and primary purpose of the church, of every congregation, is to love God with all you have. Is there any evidence to show that you have been filled with this love? The second is like it.

Love Others

Jesus instructs us to put God first – people next – ourselves last! *"Love your neighbor as yourself."* The mark of a healthy church is found in loving relationships. When people give of themselves to the care of each other, something marvelous happens. But we cannot love each other if we put ourselves first. A wonderful teaching is found in Luke: our Lord is approached by would be disciples who promise to follow Him wherever He goes. In this passage we get the idea that life is all about Christ, not about ourselves:

> *"As they were walking along the road, a man said to him, "I will follow you wherever you go." Jesus replied, "Foxes have holes and birds of the air have nests, but the Son of Man has no place to lay his head." He said to another man, "Follow me." But the man replied, "Lord, first let me go and bury my father." Jesus said to him, "Let the dead bury their own dead, but you go and proclaim the kingdom of God." Still another said, "I will follow you, Lord; but first let me go back and say good-by to my family." Jesus replied, "No one who puts his hand to the plow and looks back is fit for service in the kingdom of God""* (Luke 9:57-62)

At least they got the "follow" part right. After all, it is following Christ that leads us into the presence of the Father. In my Bible I have circled three words found in this passage. They are the words "Lord," "me", and "first." We cannot say, "Lord, I will follow you, but me first." No, it is not about me, it's about making Him our first priority, followed by loving His people. We need to teach our congregations that our lives are to be focused not on ourselves but God first, followed by our neighbor. If we say, "Lord, me first" or "But first me," then we are living according to the view of the world and this makes it impossible to be in genuine loving relationships with each other. These would be followers of Jesus were suffering from a selfish worldview.

The highest ideal of a non-Christian worldview is to be completely satisfied in one's self, called "self actualization." Our educational system is teaching our children a very different set of priorities from those taught by Christ. By way of example, take "Maslow's hierarchy of needs" which clearly places "self actualization" as the highest ideal. This theory is the predominant teaching of our schools of business, sociology, and psychology. It is influencing everything about our culture and how people conduct the business of living, and it is wrong!

> In 1943 Abraham Maslow, one of the founding fathers of humanist approaches to management, wrote an influential paper that set out five fundamental human needs and their hierarchical nature. They are quoted and taught so widely now that many people perceive this model as the definitive set of needs and do not look further.[6]

Maslow's theory has become so widely accepted, even by Christians, that it is considered normative in our educational system. According to this view, the mission is to serve "me first." Serving others comes only as a means of getting what we want. In fact, the only way to be fully actualized or happy as a human being is to focus on your own wants and desires, manipulating people and providing for their needs only when it serves the purpose of helping you get what you want. No wonder Wall Street is in such a mess if this is what our business students are being taught. In this view, no God exists, and even if you believe that He does, you only pray for the things you want. Usually you don't pray at all in this view, unless you did not get what you wanted! After all, the world would have you believe that you are the center of importance, not God. Truth becomes relative and based primarily on whatever it takes to get what I deserve so that I can be happy. I saw a billboard on I75 in Detroit one day. It was an ad for a hospital with the caption, "You deserve a doctor from this hospital." I imagined a pedophile driving up that highway, seeing the sign and saying to himself, "That's right, I do deserve it!"

Consider the chart depicting the "hierarchy of needs."[7] Note the emphasis not on respecting or serving others, but rather on obtaining respect from others. The second highest item on this list is based on getting something from others, rather than on the giving of yourself to others. According to this teaching, the very highest ideal that man can achieve is to be self satisfied. It's all about me. Scripture calls this way of living sin, which is the primary reason why we were separated from God. It is why we need a Savior to rescue us from our self centeredness and restore us to Him.

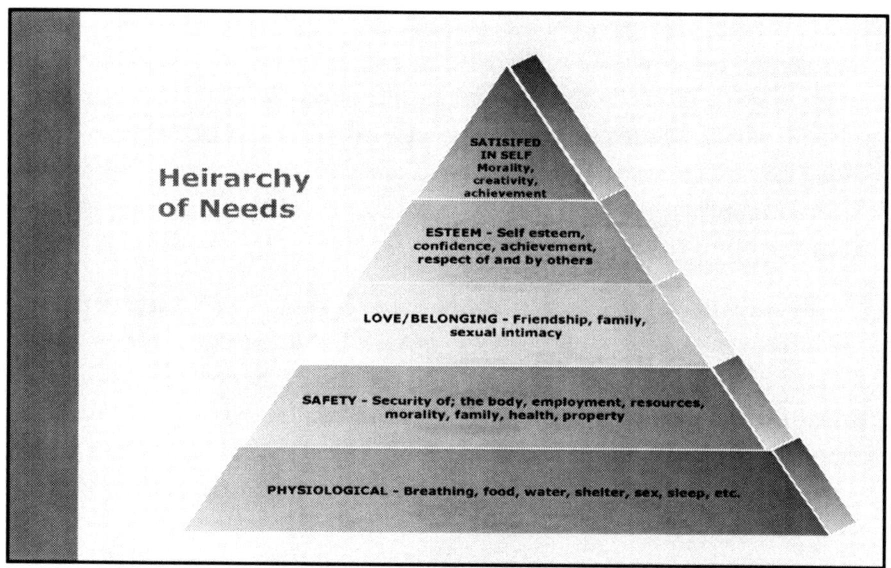

This view is the opposite of the commandment given by Christ, which teaches us to love God first and people next, putting ourselves last. The truth is this: the highest ideal and our main source of happiness come from serving God and people. It becomes our responsibility to demonstrate, by how we work together, a life that places God first, people next and ourselves last. This way of living is visibly different from the world view that surrounds us.

And this way of living will be demonstrated by how the leaders of a church work with each other and with employees and volunteers. If the work environment is causing stress and creating high turnover, there is something very wrong at the leadership level. I submit that a people living as Christ instructed will be noticed and will also attract others to join them! Isn't that the point? Isn't our faith in Christ supposed to change how we live, giving us true joy in living through service to each other?

Jesus provided the remaining three purposes when He gave The Great Commission:

> "*"All authority in heaven and on earth has been given to me. Therefore go and make disciples of all nations, baptizing them in the name of the Father and of the Son and of the Holy Spirit, and teaching them to obey everything I have commanded you. And surely I am with you always, to the very end of the age."* (Matthew 28:18-20)

A reason and purpose lie behind the Biblical idea of elder led congregational government. We need to understand what Christ wants us to accomplish as we do life together in His name. It starts with our love of God, which, in turn, triggers a response of service to His people. When leadership encourages a loving and healthy environment for the "saints" to have with each other, God will add to their number by attracting people from the world to join them.

By functioning together in obedience to Scripture we greatly improve the effectiveness of our ministry while assuring its success. In this most famous of "mission statements," we find the three remaining components of our fivefold mission and purpose. They can be summarized by the words evangelism, identification and discipleship.[8] One should be familiar with them in order to gain insight into why Biblical elders and teamwork are so important.

Evangelism:

"Therefore go and make disciples of all nations,"

Evangelism is the first component of the mission. A little grammar should be considered here as we consider the difference between a verb and a verbal participle.[9] In Matthew 28:18-19 the original Greek used four key words translated "go," "make disciples," "baptizing" and "teaching." However, only one main verb (the action) occurs in this passage. The other three words are verbal participles placed there to help us understand how the main action will be achieved. When I teach the class, "How to Study the Bible using the Inductive Method," I like to ask the students a question: "What is the main verb or action word in this passage of Scripture?" Usually I get the answer, "Go." It is not the verb.

The word "go" comes from the Greek word πορευθέντες (pronounced poreuthentes). It is not a verb, but rather a verbal participle and its function here is to illustrate a life focused on living for God, which has the impact of making disciples as one is going.[10] In other words, it represents an attitude of concern for the unsaved, a heart for sharing the good news, a life whose relationship with others flows out of a love for God. Our focus will be illustrated by the way we live. The main verb is not "go," but rather the word translated "make disciples" from μαθητεύσατε (pronounced matheteusate). All four of these words are in the form of a command: this form emphasizes that Christ expects us to live a certain way. He commands us to go through life in a manner that gets certain results. Further, the Greek used a type of verb not found in English, called aorist. All four words are in the aorist tense, which has the probable meaning, "It will just happen from time to time." In other words, the Lord commands and expects that as we go about living our lives, the result will be to "make disciples."

Salvation is presumed to have already taken place in this mission statement. Reaching the lost is the presumed result of the "saints" living together in loving relationships. This does not come from some corporate culture that uses gimmicks to attract people to come to church, but rather from believers being equipped to live for Christ. From time to time we will look over our shoulders and see others following us on the path of discipleship as we follow Christ. Why? Because the Holy Spirit is visible in our daily living and He is convicting others of sin and their need for a Savior.

The question becomes this, "When a local citizen observes you as you go about living, do they see a model of Christ?" After all, discipleship implies being a person who follows Rabbi Jesus for the purpose of becoming like Him and sharing His concern for the salvation of others. And this is evident in how the saints do life together as modeled at the leadership level. In the first century, the disciples of a rabbi were committed to becoming like their rabbi. They were called his "Talmidim."[11] They were expected to study the rabbi's words and learn to mimic his ways: to pray like him, act like him, and live like him. The way a disciple lived life was a direct reflection of the one they were following. So it is for us. If we are to be disciples of Jesus, we need to learn to walk the walk we talk. We are instructed first to love God with all we have and care for each other in response to that love. In doing so, others will see in us a life that is different, meaningful, and real. A favorite old song of mine has the verse, "They will know we are Christians by our love." As a result of this love it should happen that others will choose to follow Christ also. So how are you doing at the leadership level in your church? If your people are suffering stress and burnout coupled with high turnover you should take a serious look at the model being displayed by your leadership.

In the eighteenth verse of this passage, known as "The Great Commission," we are provided with the third component of the mission: evangelism. Is the Holy Spirit in you convicting others around you of the need for a Savior? Who is following you? Who are you following and obeying? How are you living, especially in relationship with other believers? Are you even going? If you have the Great Commandment right, loving God with all your heart, then it should follow that your love for others will be seen as you ***go*** about living.

Identification:

> *"baptizing them in the name of the father and of the Son and of the Holy Spirit,"*

Here we find the second instance of a verbal participle, rather than a verb. It further describes how Jesus expects disciples to be made. It is wrapped in an understanding of the word "baptizing." The second component of the mission and the fourth purpose of the church is "identification." It is our identification with the death, burial, and resurrection of Christ that allows us to receive salvation. Accepting the gift of salvation by believing in the "one of a kind" Son of God and believing that He was raised from the dead is the only way to be safe from judgment by receiving forgiveness (Romans 10:9). We first identify with Christ to be saved. It is the only way into heaven: *Jesus answered, "I am the way and the truth and the life. No one comes to the Father except through me* (John 14:6.)

Baptism by itself does not offer salvation. We are saved by grace through faith alone. Baptism illustrates our identification with Christ, accompanied by the opportunity to make a public profession of faith that says, "I believe in Jesus for the forgiveness of my sins and from this day forward I have put to death my old way of living as I commit to living life anew in obedience to Him." Baptism is an act of obedience with a commitment to follow Jesus coupled with a commitment from the "saints" to help you accomplish it. It is followed by a desire to go and tell people about your decision as you show them the power of a life lived for Christ, in relationship with others and obedience to servant leadership.

Many churches practice a believer's baptism while others infant baptism. The one expects a person to follow their profession of faith with baptism as a statement to the church of their decision to follow Christ. The other gathers the church in infant baptism followed by a commitment to raise that child to live the Christian life. Both persuasions offer some beautiful tradition and have many examples of true believers working to follow and obey Jesus. And yet, in both cases many people fall into a habit of following their tradition as just a ritual that one does to be part of church. Like the Hebrews of old, a system that becomes rote or habit for the sake of following rules is of no value to the Christian life.

I am comfortable with either tradition, though my personal preference is for a believer's baptism, in which salvation is followed by full immersion as one makes the commitment to be a disciple..

But in the larger scheme of things I don't think it makes a difference in terms of salvation. No matter which persuasion you follow, did you know that the process of making a pickle involves the idea of "baptism?" It does! Once you have "baptized" a cucumber into the vinegar and spices, in time it becomes a pickle. It can never again be a cucumber! It is changed forever and everyone can tell the difference between a cucumber and a pickle. The change takes time and commitment and is made in us when we choose to become a follower of Jesus by making a profession of our faith while making steady progress toward changing how we think and live. Baptism or confirmation is public because the way of the cross is public. The people in Jesus' day who carried their cross down a very public road to the place of their crucifixion were a spectacle for all to see. They stood out among the local citizens. You could tell they were different. When we accept Christ for our salvation the expected result is to follow Him down a road that demonstrates a way of living very different from the world's way of living. As such, in our new identity we should be very different from those who do not believe. Are you a cucumber or a pickle?

A few years ago I made a trip to Greece and Turkey on a study tour of the places where the Apostle Paul planted churches. We visited some wonderful places, including archeological sites at Corinth, Athens, Ephesus, and Mars Hill. We ended the trip in Istanbul, Turkey. One evening after dinner, our guide invited us to walk downtown. The crowd of people was thick as our group followed him through the streets and up a hill to a very large park surrounded by buildings and sidewalks and roads, and did I say "*lots* of people?" I stopped for a moment to purchase roasted chestnuts from a street vendor, and when I looked up, my group was gone – hidden in the crowd! Having not been paying attention to where I was going, there was no way I could find the hotel on my own. Panic gripped me as I, surrounded by Arabs, walked quickly in the direction they had been traveling. They were nowhere in sight. I was approached by an Arab sporting a braided beard, turban, and robe. He had made eye contact with me from across the street. "Oh, no, now what?" I thought. He did not stop his approach until his belly was touching my belly, which added to my discomfort.

As I looked into his bright blue eyes, he said, in heavily accented English, "You look troubled, my American friend; may I help you?" I thought, "How did he know I was American?" I said "Yes, please, I lost my tour group and need to find them." He laughed and pointed down the street and said, "You mean them?" I looked where he was pointing, and, sure enough, my little band of Americans were there, walking down the street and sticking out like a sore thumb among the throng of Arabs that surrounded them. I laughed with him at the spectacle my friends made among his fellow Arabs. He took one of my roasted chestnuts as payment, delivered a smile that I will never forget, and patted me on the back as I rushed to meet them.

It's like that in our identification with Christ. We should be changed. We should live in such a way as to stick out like a sore thumb among the citizens of the world who live where we are walking. If we blend in, it is probably because we are living like them instead of like a disciple of Christ. Have you been changed? Are you a member of His "Talmidim?"

In baptism we are put under the water, identifying ourselves with His death, burial, and resurrection; it is as if we say, "Not my will any longer but yours be done." It is a symbol of the death of our selfishness. No longer do we say, "Me first," but rather, "God first," from now on. Rising up out of the water identifies us with new birth and new life in Christ. Have you been transformed into a pickle yet? Now consider the last of the five purposes of the church.

Discipleship:

"and teaching them to obey everything I have commanded you."

The word disciple comes to us from the Greek word μαθητής (pronounced mathetes). The word is rendered "disciple or student" in its noun form. It is rendered "to learn" in the verb form. Its primary meaning comes from the idea of being committed to learning as a student. The implication in the New Testament is to become the follower of a Rabbi, dedicated to learning from him how to live by becoming like him. In Jesus' day the Rabbi was primarily responsible for teaching the people how to live as God intended.

They were focused on the application of Scripture because they desired to live rightly before God. Different rabbis had different ideas on how to apply Scripture.

For example, one rabbi would allow a person to walk a certain distance from home on the Sabbath, but another would not. One would allow a person to rescue an animal who fell down a well, while another would not. One would allow divorce in a situation in which another would not. One would help a person in need; another would not. Each rabbi taught his approach to living correctly according to his interpretation of Old Testament Scripture. The system of learning in Jesus' day was an oral one. Few copies of Scripture existed. A local synagogue was fortunate to have a single copy from which the rabbi would teach. The interpretations of the rabbis were eventually written down, becoming a system of learning called the "Mishnah."[12]

Each rabbi had a system for living, a school of thought which was called his "yoke."[13] It was within this system that Jesus told His disciples,

> *"Take my yoke upon you and learn from me, for I am gentle and humble in heart, and you will find rest for your souls. For my yoke is easy and my burden is light"* (Matt 11:29-30).

Our rabbi is Jesus and He really does know how to live rightly before God because He is Lord and wrote the instructions! If we learn to live as He did, we will live a righteous life. In fact, in Luke, Jesus used the same word translated "disciple" in our mission statement, but in this case rendered "student:" *"A student is not above his teacher, but everyone who is fully trained will be like his teacher"* (Luke 6:40). We cannot help someone live correctly unless we first become a disciple of Christ and learn how to live by following Him. By first addressing the sin in our own life, we will see clearly to help another address the sin in theirs. In so doing, the fruit that is produced in our life will be the evidence that proves we are His disciples. A bad tree cannot produce good fruit (Luke 6:39-49).

Now consider what Jesus said when He called His very first disciples to "follow" Him saying,

> *"Repent, for the kingdom of heaven is near." As Jesus was walking beside the Sea of Galilee, he saw two brothers, Simon called Peter and his brother Andrew. They were casting a net into the lake, for they*

> *were fishermen. "Come, follow me," Jesus said, "and I will make you fishers of men"* (Matthew 4:17-19).

The word "repent" conveys the idea "to change your mind or change how you think about how to live." Here Jesus demonstrates exactly the same goal that other rabbis had at the time: teach people how to live righteously through application of Scripture. The problem is that no one, regardless of how hard they try, can do so perfectly and earn their way into heaven. Trying to follow all the rules and regulations of a rabbi became a heavy burden. Legalism may teach a person what to do but it does not provide salvation. We make too many mistakes, and when you've made just one, even in your thoughts (Matthew 5:28), "Oops, too late; here comes the judge."

Jesus invited his first disciples, His "Talmidim," to enter His school, put on His yoke, and learn from Him the real way to live for God. His way does not require us to do anything to earn salvation because He faced the Judge and paid the price of failure for us. His way also carries an expectation that we change how we live in response to salvation as we dwell temporarily in the "enemy occupied territory" (C.S. Lewis) of this world. A true disciple of Jesus is serious about learning the Word of God, applying it to his or her life, and changing how he or she lives by conforming to or becoming like Jesus gradually over time and showing others the way. The entire process is fueled by our love of God and others. Therefore, a disciple is a student who is serious about living for Jesus. One of my favorite theology professors summed it up well, "A student learns what his teacher knows but a disciple becomes what his Master is."[14]

Jesus trained his first group of twelve how to follow, which is another way of saying "obey," and they in turn taught others. Those who abide in His teaching by loving each other and doing what Jesus commands will also train others, producing much fruit while the rest will be cast aside (John 15). At every place where a church was established the original apostles passed on the mantle of their authority to elders who were expected to shepherd the flock of God by leading them in the way of Christ and teaching God's Word so the "Talmidim" could obey all that Christ has commanded and live a righteous life. This is why the leadership team of your church must demonstrate loving and caring and equipping relationships among the saints to be successful. Love and care for the "saints" must be demonstrated at the top. And this will create a culture that will not only reach the lost, but also turn them into trained disciples.

Let me make one final point on being a disciple. Jesus expects us to deny ourselves, take up our cross and follow Him (Matthew 16:24-25). In this context, the point is that it is not about us, it's about Him. We are not to live for ourselves, but for Christ (God first, me last). He expects us to deny the things of this world and its way of living and its plan and purpose for our lives. Instead we are to put this worldly way of living to death and learn to follow His plan and purpose. After all, we cannot know how to make right decisions without Him. He knows; we do not. The cross represents an instrument of death. In our identification with Christ we die to ourselves in order to live for Him. This is what it means to take up our cross: put to death our old way, our old self, and live life for Him - "repent and become fishers of men!"

Thus, the purpose of the church and mission of Christ is divided into five components. First, **love God:** We cannot achieve the mission if we do not love God with everything we have, putting Him first. Remember, worship is the same as recognizing His worth as highest, above everything. Next, **love others:** Our response to the knowledge of what He has done for us on the cross should be demonstrated by our love for each other. After that, the primary action in our mission is represented by the verb "make disciples." It is accomplished by the verbal participles "Go" (**Evangelism**), "Baptizing" (**Identification**), and "Teaching" (**Discipleship**).

Again, the five purposes and our mission: love God, love others, evangelism, identification and discipleship.

Perhaps we can begin to understand why the elder, referred to here as an overseer, is required to have the ability to teach: *"Now the overseer must be above reproach, the husband of one wife, temperate, self controlled, respectable, hospitable, **able to teach**," (*emphasis mine, 1Tim 3:2). The elder derives the authority to lead God's people from God's Word. Dare I postulate that the New Testament elder is the modern day Christian equivalent of the rabbi? Yes! Rabbi means "master and teacher!" Jesus is our Rabbi (Master) and the elder is our rabbi, teacher. Teaching the word of God should be the elders' highest priority.

Jesus, the "hinge of history," changes everything!

The Resurrection is the event that makes Jesus the "hinge of history." This momentous event brought much more than the payment of a ransom to redeem fallen man from captivity. It is also the cosmic spiritual event that opened up the future for the entire created order. The Old Testament told of a time to come when a "new thing" would be done by God in a time referred to as "the last days." Jesus' authoritative message brought a new element to our understanding of prophecy; specifically, the kingdom age expected to come was now present. By way of example, Jesus said, *"But if I drive out demons by the Spirit of God, then the kingdom of God has come upon you"* (Matt 12:28). The implication is that we are living in a life between ages, a life between times. The "Church age" exists between the age that was and the age that will be after Christ returns.[15] During this age in which we live, Scripture prescribes a system for living that includes elders showing us the way while we do life together for Christ and await His return.

> As participants with Christ in His death, burial, resurrection, and exaltation (Rom 6:3-7; Col 2:12, 30; 3:1-5; Eph 2:5-6), believers have experienced the "powers of the age to come (Heb 6:5), but they continue to live temporally in this age. Thus, Christian existence is constantly subject to the tension between the "already" and the "not yet," between the claims of the new creation in Christ and the threat of evil in this age (Rom 12:2; 1Cor 1:20; 3:18; 2Cor 4:4; 5:17; Eph 1:21; 2:2 Titus 2:12).
>
> The struggle of the individual believer is but a microcosm of the overlapping of the ages; those on whom "the fulfillment of the ages has come (1Cor 10:11) engage the conflict of old man and new man, of flesh and the Spirit, of death and life. The interim period of existence between the times, called the "last days" or the "last hour" (Acts 2:17; Rom 13:12; Heb 1:2; Jas 5:3; 1Pet 1:5; 1John 2:18), stretches from the first advent of Christ to His parousia *(arrival)*. Only at the Lord's coming and the resurrection day will the triumph be made complete (1Thess 4:13-18; 1Cor 1:8; 15:50-58; Phil 3:20).
>
> *The People of God.* The cross and resurrection of Christ is the twofold sign under which His followers live. By His cross, they have died to this world and share in His sufferings, but by His resurrection, they live to serve in power: "For the sufferings of Christ flow over into our lives, so also through Christ our comfort overflows" (2Cor 1:5; 4:14; 13:4; Gal 6:14). Because the dawning

of the new age did not abolish the hostile forces of this present age, the messianic woes endured by Christ spill over into His body, the church (Col 1:24), which suffers with Him and for His names sake (Rom 8:17-18; Phil 1:29; 3:10; 1Pet 4:12-16). The "god of this age" stands against the church's witness (2Cor 4:4), just as the "rulers of this age" (1Cor 2:6,8) through human ignorance crucified the Lord of glory. This fallen order is ruled by principalities and powers who have been vanquished by Christ (Col 2:15; Eph 1:20-23) but engage in warfare against the people of God (Eph 2:2; 6:12; Gal 4:3, 9; Col 1:16; 2:8; 1John 2:18; 4:3; 2Thes 2:1-11; Rev 13:1-10). In the midst of this battle, there is necessary suffering – not only passive resistance to the onslaught of the demonic powers but also, as J.C. Beker puts it, "suffering as a result of active Christian engagement with the world," wherein the church carries out God's redemptive mission.

Not even the "gates of Hades" will be able to stand against the mission of Christ's church (Matt 16:18; 1Cor 15:25). That Jesus deliberately chose twelve apostles emphasizes the continuity of His followers with the congregation of Israel, not simply a new Israel that supersedes the old, but in fact the true Israel, one that is gathered to the Messiah. The choice of the term "assembly" (Gk. Ekklesia, 115 occurrences) for the Messiah's people carries in it the secret of the church's mission: This people is gathered to the Messiah by confession and empowered by Him to be scattered in the earth (Acts 1:6-8). "The chief characteristic of the new people of God gathered together by Jesus is their awareness of the boundlessness of God's grace."[16]

How is it possible to understand what has been accomplished for us and not love God with everything we have? The mighty work of Christ on the cross has created an opportunity for all people to be restored to a personal relationship with God, if they accept it. He bridges the gap between man and God caused by sin with His own body and blood. In the sacrifice of Christ, the door to our prison cell has been unlocked and all we have to do is open it and walk out, followed by learning as His disciple to change how we live. This is the foundation of the Christian faith and becomes the reason why Christ provided the mission in the first place. Accomplishing the mission requires an organization that functions well.

Building Well on the Foundation Requires Organization

The Apostle Paul speaks of this foundation and refers to the importance of how we build upon it saying,

> *"By the grace God has given me, I laid a foundation as an expert builder, and someone else is building on it. But each one should be careful how he builds"* (1Cor 3:10).

Can you imagine any kind of building project that involves the combined work and effort of a lot of people, but has no organization or hierarchy, no leaders in charge and no people willing to follow? Imagine a group of fifty people who come together some Saturday to build a house. There is a blueprint but nobody knows how to read it. There is no recognized foreman or boss, so everyone just picks up a board and a nail and starts putting things together, making separate decisions about what is right, apart from any authority. What would the result be? A mess, as well as an argument!

The Bible has provided a structure of organization that we are expected to use. We need some form of organization under Christ that builds on the foundation effectively. The model of government established by Christ borrowed heavily from the model in place at the time of His coming. He placed twelve apostles in charge of the early church, and they, in turn, planted churches and appointed elders to lead those churches.

As the church grew, the work of serving became a hindrance to the elders' ministry of prayer and teaching the Word of God. The result was another church office: the office of deacon. This situation is probably alluded to in Acts chapter 6, and though the word "deacon" was not used, other words, implying "servant," were. People are like sheep and tend to wander and stray (1Pet 2:25; Matt 9:36). They need to be led by a shepherd, described as a "servant leader" (1Pet 5:3). As people make the commitment to discipleship and are led into a mature faith, with knowledge of the Word and service to each other, some will become leaders. Some will receive a call to become elders, some deacons, and some ministry leaders, in a variety of jobs that are under the oversight of the elders, who serve under the authority of Christ. Everyone is expected to serve together in love, as the chosen of God, a royal priesthood, a holy nation, belonging to Him (1Pet 2:9).

We find clear and specific pastoral instructions regarding the conduct of people in the church in the writings of Paul, Peter, James and John. They testify to an apostolic tradition that existed at the time of Christ and is essential to the Christian way of living. The letter of James is all about having a faith that actually works, and faith requires obedience to do what the Word of God says, even when we do not understand why. We can, in faith, trust the Word of God even when it makes us uncomfortable. In the three letters of John we are given various tests of truth, faith, and love which are contrasted with the spirit of error. It is through the knowledge, understanding, and application of God's Word that life may be lived correctly as a disciple. In Paul's "Pastoral Epistles," we find specific instructions regarding the elders' responsibility to teach the Word accurately. In the elder rests the authority to lead and shepherd the people who would become disciples.

Evangelical Christians refer loosely to two systems of church government: "Congregational Rule" and "Elder Rule." Which one is correct? Scripture seems to portray a balance between the two that I will call "Elder Led Congregational Government."

A variety of governmental systems have developed from within these two general forms. The key to success, regardless of what you may call your system, is having gifted people with the Scriptural character qualifications in place to lead and a people who are willing to follow.

CHAPTER 2

"Is my church producing sufficient fruit--that of new believers, being baptized and becoming engaged in God's word and learning to be obedient disciples for Christ who are serious about helping others become disciples too-- so that I can have confidence to believe we are successful at accomplishing the mission?"

The Biblical system for church government allows flexibility.

Extremism in any form or system of church government produces problems that tend to reduce the effectiveness of a congregation and limit its ability to achieve the mission Christ has given. Scripture provides flexibility for believers to respond to the urgings of the Holy Spirit, including the way in which government is carried out within the local church. Each congregation has its particular gifts, resources, people, and needs. Each congregation exists in a community having its own unique "culture," and the congregation must respond to that culture in ways that are effective at reaching the lost with the Gospel message. I have observed a trend that is causing churches to attempt duplication of a process or program that seems to work at another church in a different location. Often, a church will achieve significant success at reaching the lost because they came up with something that was a real fit for the culture in which they were ministering while also maximizing the gifts available to them by the people serving there. The Holy Spirit will often lead people into a way of accomplishing ministry that works well for them. But, this does not mean the idea will be readily transferable to your church.

You have your own community and culture to work with. You have a group of committed believers that are unique to you. Since every person is a unique creation of God, especially gifted with his or her own unique combination of spiritual gifts, temperament and experience it follows that your church will be unique as well. You have a personality made from the combination of people who call you "my church." You need to find a way to achieve the mission with your people and within your culture and what worked elsewhere may not work for you. It is not about duplicating process but rather developing people to maturity so ministry will be achieved. Any successful organization will change and adapt to meet the changing needs of the organization over time. We might say it is important to be culturally relevant without compromising Scripture. Church history clearly demonstrates the church's ability to adapt. At the same time, Scripture describes, both in direct and indirect ways, a system that provides a model for each local congregation to follow. It is within the confines of the Biblical guidelines for government that this flexibility should exist.

New Testament elders are called to be servant leaders who guide the congregation forward, using Scripture as the authority for their direction, setting a personal example for a congregation to follow, and equipping them to actually do works of service. I believe Scripture supports the idea of a balanced form of government: one that allows elders to lead and the congregation to participate with them. The reason for having trained leaders work with the congregation is so that believers can be taught to disciple others even as they together achieve the mission.

The Scriptural model is a fellowship of loving people who, being guided by the Holy Spirit, work in cooperation with and submission to their leaders. Elders have the responsibility to lead, and congregations are expected to follow and also obey (Heb 13:17). Servant leadership, caring teamwork, flexibility, and fellowship are necessary underlying ingredients. Sheep will simply not follow a shepherd they do not trust. It thus becomes important to understand God's expectation of and requirements for elders, who will ultimately be held accountable for the way in which they fulfill their duties, and to understand the organizational structure under which Christ expects them to operate.

My goal in writing this book is to remove some of the misunderstanding, misinformation and fear associated with the Scriptural model, which clearly vests management and oversight authority in a person (or persons) commonly referred to as "elder." Elders are expected to work in cooperation with their congregation as servant leaders. At the heart of the issue is the simple concept of obedience to Christ and obedience to Scripture. Problems and obstacles that make ministry for Christ ineffective are always overcome when people stop doing things "their own way" and choose to obey His Word. Since He has provided a clear and effective organizational model, it follows that a congregation of believers would achieve better results by following it. The mission we have already discussed will be accomplished more effectively when we operate according to Scripture instead of following some other man made instructions.

A Very Important Question:

At this point it becomes important to ask yourself a very important question: "Is my church producing sufficient fruit--that of new believers, being baptized and becoming engaged in God's word and learning to be obedient disciples for Christ who are serious about helping others become disciples too-- so that I can have confidence to believe we are successful at accomplishing the mission?"

In other words, are we maximizing our potential for Christ? Is our love of God evident in our love for each other? Are we achieving the fivefold mission and purpose of Christ? Be honest in your assessment here. Growth in numbers does not mean you are achieving success. However, if the answer is "yes," perhaps your system is fine and it would not surprise me to learn that you are using a form of government that follows, or at least resembles, an elder led model (regardless of what your church may call it). If your answer is "no," you should examine your current form of government and the relationships that exist between leaders and members. Perhaps it needs to be changed or more clearly defined. The Word of God should be our source of authority and the means by which we test our decisions and claims of truth. Today, more than ever, we need to learn how to refrain from taking things from our culture and applying them to Scripture. Instead, we need to learn from Scripture and apply it to our culture.

Two Prevailing Views: The Good, the Bad and the Ugly of Each

Two primary forms of government exist in Protestant churches, though they exist along a spectrum, sometimes tending to one extreme or the other. These forms, at their extreme, are in direct opposition to one another. Both sides present arguments to support their position. The first view falls under the general heading of "Congregationalism," and the second view falls under the general heading of "Elder Led Congregations." From discussions I have had with church members and leaders from both sides, it is obvious that the topic is one that invokes strong emotional reactions.

Congregationalism:

In congregationalism, management and oversight authority are held in the local assembly, free from outside forces or hierarchy. Its original and noble purpose was to move the church toward restoration of early Biblical principles that encourages all believers to take part in ministry. The movement toward this form of government came into being in reaction to extremism within church government during the time of the Reformation. During and after the Reformation, congregationalism became a rallying cry for the "Free Church" who wished to move away from state (government) sponsored control over local congregations. It was a movement away from individual pastors or bishops who "lorded it over" local assemblies, leading in an authoritative way rather than in a serving way.

In this form, each local assembly is free to choose for themselves how they will be governed, what mission activities will be their focus, and how to respond effectively to the unique cultural influences within their community. Most of the modern Congregational movements made their protests against the churches of the Reformation, strongly entrenched as state churches. Further, the movement objected to a developing clergy class that was quite similar to the priest class of Romanism, which the movement was interested in eliminating. The autonomy of the local church has been the battle cry of the Congregational movement for decades.[17]

It would appear, then, that congregationalism came into being as a direct response to state control over churches and an extreme form of elder rule as found in the Roman Catholic Church at that time, but still found in many protestant churches even today. The Reformation movement toward congregational rule was more political than religious. The aspect of congregationalism that goes too far is a tendency toward an attitude that de-empowers the Biblical authority of the elder and hamstrings an elder from being able to perform as Scripture intended.[18] As is always the case, when Scripture is taken out of context in reaction to one's experience or in order to support one's political views, the end result is a system that derails a Biblical view of polity and lines of authority within the church.[19]

Who has the authority in a congregational government?

> Congregationalism is a church government, which gives the congregation the final authority in the doctrine and all affairs of the church. Congregationalism is that type of church government which holds; 1) that the local church's highest authority under God and His Word resides in the collective will of the local church membership, and 2) that the responsibility for ministry also belongs to the entire local church membership.[20]

Under this model, one often finds the highest authority in the church to reside in the collective will of members, presumably working under the direction of Christ through the Holy Spirit and direction of God's Word. The Scriptural basis for this authority, it is believed, is found under the concept of "the priesthood of all believers," in which every member is expected to have leadership responsibilities.[21] There are those who would even argue that the pastoral letters themselves are nothing of the sort. Rather, these letters of Paul are prescriptions on how all members of the body should behave and they are not designed to provide instructions to leaders in general, nor elders specifically.[22] Therefore, under the authority of Christ, the collective membership is the authority by which the church should be governed. Everyone has an equal say. If taken too far, congregationalism can resemble a "government of the people, by the people and for the people."

Problems Created by this View

> You don't have to look much further than the pastor/Elder to see just how much they are trusted, followed, obeyed and empowered by the congregation. In churches where the members do not follow their Elders, where roadblocks are set up to Elders leading, the church will be stifled and unsuccessful.[23]

Many pastors are hired for a job in this system and soon find themselves having to report to a completely new board of directors who ran for office because they did not like what the pastor was doing. Somehow they believed it is their duty to become a member of the board so they can exert the authority of their faction group to stop or oust the pastor. People's politics often exert a strong influence upon their understanding of Scripture. Life experience and political leanings frequently cause a person to make Biblical interpretations that are out of context. The fact is that the politics of the world are very different from the way and will of God. Politics as it is played out on earth are against the system of sovereignty of God with the resulting obedience to Him and the structures He has provided as a blueprint for living. Care should be taken not to let polity and opinion influence the clear meaning of the Scripture.[24] In God's system there is a hierarchy that goes against a modern democratic government; this idea is particularly difficult for Americans to accept.

Other problems can develop in a system where everyone believes he or she has an equal voice or authority. New Age and postmodern thinking can infiltrate the church. Everyone is entitled to an opinion about what is true and what is not, regardless of their spiritual maturity or Biblical knowledge. Anyone can say, "I am a Christian," and then immediately asked to serve in or placed in charge of some ministry within the church. In our era of postmodernism, truth has become relative rather than absolute. Many of the people today who are being converted to Christianity are coming out of the postmodern or New Age movements or at least the influence of these ideas. Though their conversion may well be genuine, their frame of reference, experience, and preconceptions are not often changed overnight. These new members have no idea what the origins of congregationalism were or what the original intention of the movement was. These believers need to read Scripture and have it explained so that it can affect their lives and help them live differently for Christ. We call this exegetical teaching, and it is part of the job description of the elder/pastor, as we will see in later chapters. There is a big difference between these two sentences, "I know Jesus is Lord" and "I know Jesus as Lord." Knowledge of Jesus is not the same thing as submission to Jesus.

Personal experience and views of polity, especially in America, result in many churches who govern themselves like a democracy, giving power to the people. Consequently, traditional church values, such as tithing and obedience to authority outside ones' self, described in Scripture become a matter of personal interpretation. If the plain meaning of Scripture makes one uncomfortable it becomes acceptable to allegorize the meaning into something other than what was originally intended. There is little, if any, commitment to the hard work of studying Scripture, which is a requirement for one who would be a disciple. Instead, all it takes to do what you want is a majority vote.

Since the authority of a teaching elder is not acknowledged, correction of false doctrine is difficult and even impossible. If one disagrees with the Word of God, people can turn in their disobedience to modern critical scholars who teach that certain paragraphs or entire Biblical books were not intended to be in the Bible and can be disregarded. Though these results may sound outrageous, they can be clearly seen in many churches. I have personal experience with a local congregation who elected a president of the church board who was promoting a New Age program called "EST" to its members on the side. This program, developed by Werner H. Erhard, attempts to teach participants from the religion of "Zen" a way to personal transformation and enhanced power for living.[25] The program is very different from the teaching of Scripture. Nobody had a clue how the Scripture compared, let alone had the ability to respond to it. No accountability to the authority of a teaching elder existed. As of this writing, the church continues to flounder and languish.

Another potential problem is that disobedience to authority may become normal if each member believes they are the authority under Christ. If this is true, how can one explain the amount of disharmony that often exists within these churches? Where two opinions or interpretations exist, there can be only two possibilities: one is right or both are wrong. From beginning to end, Scripture discusses the need for human beings to be obedient in following Christ while loving God and each other. A model of government that allows everyone to be in authority is a model that does not effectively teach or model obedience. I observed a compelling example of this behavior in the adult Sunday school class of a local Free Church congregation. An elected leader had volunteered to teach the class, and his topic was congregational authority. He taught, and I quote,

> Members of our church are all together the authority under Christ. We need no person to function with so called 'Elder Authority.' No, if we followed leaders, who knows what could happen to us? We would become no better than a bunch of Lemmings who are in danger of running right off a cliff.

Often the "Mission and Vision Statement" (if there is one at all) is unclear in this model because the wording has to be vague and imprecise in order to appeal to all the members. Mission focus is often lost because the membership has so many different ideas about what it is. People head off in different directions based on personal opinion. The result is an ambiguous final document meaning different things to different people and often having nothing to do with accomplishing the mission given by Christ. As people attempt to become involved, some feel they have been given a mission or ministry by the Holy Spirit and wish to move forward with it. Others do not feel that the other person's ministry is necessary or worth committing resources to. Members take sides on the issue because the mission of the organization is not clear.

The person who felt passionate about something they believed God was calling them to do becomes deflated and discouraged by the process. Disagreement and even arguments over an idea cause postponements to a later date when a decision can be made after a committee has been engaged to research it further. In the meantime, members get a severe case of "being busy" without being effective at achieving the actual mission that Christ provided.

Without obedience to a shepherd leader, the flock scatters. With a clear mission statement, new ideas can be checked against the mission. If implementing the idea would further the mission, the goal should be to find a way to proceed, to find a way to say "yes" instead of "no." Extreme congregationalism breeds committees, and the best thing a committee does is to say "no." This form of government attempts to apply the polity of democracy to the church. The ideas and attitudes create unique problems for elders to deal with, not the least of which is the reality that the power associated with the office is watered down to near ineffectiveness.[26] It does not matter if you call the person an elder or a pastor. Either title is sufficient in modern times. The issue is whether they are allowed to lead.

Elder Led Congregation

Here the ultimate authority is Scripture, with an established government comprised of elders in a position where they can lead effectively, guiding the flock through expository teaching and preaching (the reading, explaining, and application of Scripture.)[27] The responsibility for rule is vested in an office that dates back to pre-Christian times and is carried into the New Testament. At all times the assumption is that this person will have significant knowledge and command of Scripture. It is the primary means of equipping people to serve in ministry and the source of an elder's authority under Christ. In Paul's instruction to Timothy he wrote,

> *"But as for you, continue in what you have learned and have become convinced of, because you know those from whom you learned it, and how from infancy you have known the holy Scriptures, which are able to make you wise for salvation through faith in Christ Jesus. All Scripture is God-breathed and is useful for teaching, rebuking, correcting and training in righteousness, so that the man of God may be thoroughly equipped for every good work"* (2Tim 3:14-17).

The one obvious change in the position of elder in the developing New Testament church was the description of specific moral character attributes combined with an ability to teach in order to be qualified to serve as one. Members of a local assembly are responsible to recognize people who have the "character" of an elder and identify those who are functioning among them as a shepherd. In my opinion, it takes one to know one. Therefore, elders themselves should be significantly involved in the process of identifying fellow elders from within the congregation. In fact, it is demonstrated in Scripture that elders were appointed first by Christ and then by fellow elders (Mark 3:15; 1 Timothy 2:7; Titus 1:5; Acts 14:23).

Oversight is a spiritual matter and it is the spiritual people, with the appropriate character qualifications and knowledge of Scripture, who will own as a steward in heart and conscience the members of a particular flock whom God has called them to shepherd. It is a great departure from the will of God in Christian churches to see national systems of religion where rulers are permitted to "lord it over a congregation" because they were appointed by a Pope, or by a king, or the advice of some political party, or by a congregation themselves.[28] No, this is not the intent of Scripture with regard to elders and their authority. An authoritative senior pastor and staff who conveys the message, "My way or the highway" is hardly demonstrating a Biblical model. Above all, the elder is a servant leader who models Christ like behavior for his flock to follow and this attitude should be evident among the people he manages at the top. The elder loves God, loves others, and is committed to the Great Commission which presumes the importance of salvation but emphasis the development of true disciples.

The "Elder Led Congregational Government" is the clear teaching of Scripture. An effective model will have trusting relationships, obedience to authority, empowerment to serve, and cooperation and caring teamwork within the entire assembly, as the Scripture clearly describes. Management is part of the duty of an "overseer." Manage well!

Who has the Authority in an Elder Led Church?

In this system, authority under Christ is vested in an office of government that is occupied by an elder (or elders) who is (or are) called by God and recognized by the congregation. The number of elders is not prescribed in Scripture but there is often a plurality of them in a congregation. This would be due, in part, to the number of people to be shepherded. The authority of an elder is to be obeyed by members of the congregation, and God will hold them accountable for their actions (Heb 13:17). Since the elder is responsible for management oversight of the local assembly, there is naturally authority associated with their duties. However (and this is important), the way in which an elder is to exercise that authority is described by the word translated as "shepherd." We get the word from the Greek ποιμήν (pronounced poimen) which is translated at times "shepherd" and at times "pastor." It is a verb or action word that tells us what the elder does! In modern times we have made it a noun and use it as a title. In the Bible, it appears as a noun most often when it is referring to Christ. The elder is charged with the task of "rule" by functioning as a pastor or shepherd. To shepherd is what the elder does.

In 1 Timothy 5:17 Paul describes the elder and uses a word translated as "rule" or "direct". It comes from the word προΐστημι (pronounced proistemi) and has the meaning "to stand before" or "take the lead." The shepherd in Scripture never drives the sheep but goes before them, ruling, leading, and guiding, but not with a heavy hand. It is the same with spiritual shepherds, also known as elders. They have authority to do their God ordained ministry of overseeing, teaching, and shepherding. People cannot appoint elders to the position; they can only acknowledge it. It is a gift of God, and it is from God that they derive their authority.

Their character qualifications and spiritual gifts should be recognized and their ministry accepted with love and gratitude (1 Thess 5:12-13). Members should place themselves in subjection to those who serve as leaders (1 Cor 16:15-16) and obey their leadership without grumbling or criticism (Heb 13:17). Needless criticism lessens their authority and leaves nothing in its place. They are to be treated as fathers and not rebuked (1Tim. 5:1), and no accusation is to be received against them except when there are two or three eyewitnesses (1Tim. 5:9).[29]

Problems created by this view

Elders or Pastors sometimes abuse their position. Sometimes they rule a congregation without serving them or cooperating with or loving them. Some rule their staff and people with a heavy hand that creates an environment of stress. Others are sometimes appointed on the basis of being a nice person, rather than on their ability to teach Scripture accurately. If careful attention is not paid to the moral and character requirements of a person selected to function as an elder, an abuse of power and authority may result.

Many types of managers work in the business world. Some managers take a top down "do as I say" approach that may work well in the business community but does not fit with God's system of management. This problem of authoritarian leadership may well be the reason behind the change in emphasis in the New Testament toward the character and duties of an elder rather than the experience or gifts of an elder. Just because a member is an experienced manager in the business community does not mean he is qualified to become an elder (or a deacon, for that matter). Yet, as part of selecting an elder or pastor, members sometimes look more at what a person does in the world rather than how they act and function among the body.

Elders are not to act as if they were the "Grand Poopah" or something. Jesus said it best when he addressed those He selected to be the first elders;

> *"The kings of the Gentiles lord it over them; and those who exercise authority over them call themselves Benefactors. But you are not to be like that. Instead, the greatest among you should be like the youngest, and the one who rules like the one who serves."* (Luke 22:25-26).

This does not mean we shouldn't borrow from modern human resources management. Be careful, though, to compare a system with Scripture before implementing it. Some managers function in the business world as facilitators, team leaders, servants, and coaches. Their results are often excellent and produce a Biblical example of the kind of leadership expected of an elder. In this, you may do well to study some modern forms of organizational leadership. The important thing to know is that leaders who give orders rather than serve others, who boss rather than guide, create an atmosphere of tension and friction. They hurt people's feelings, negatively affect moral, and reduce ministry effectiveness.

Another problem that can develop in the elder led model is that people in the congregation sometimes get lazy and let their pastors do all the work. Pastors/Elders are often passionate about their ministry and actively involved in their work. For the most part, your pastor understands the mission, loves God, loves you and wants to help you grow. In some cases the congregation is happy to let the pastor do all the work! We have already defined the fivefold mission of Christ as *Love God, Love others, Evangelism, Identification and Discipleship*, which is everyone's responsibility! The pastor's job is to equip **the congregation** to do it by teaching the members what and why, by showing them how and doing it with them, and by deploying them to do it! In fact, it is in these three things that we can derive the three primary job categories of the elder: teaching/preaching, shepherding/pastoring, and overseeing/managing. I will explain this more fully in the coming chapters.

Though people may regularly attend church and be involved with the daily busy stuff of church (pot lucks, bulletins, cleaning, committee meetings, etc), these same people often let the pastoral leaders accomplish the actual mission. It is so much easier to stay in one's personal comfort zone than to move out into the world and minister to people who do not know Christ as their Savior. So, the leader becomes the one who is expected by members to perform this function. The Biblical model, in contrast, calls for every member to be responsible for the work of ministry, to produce fruit, and to be faithful. Listen to what Paul taught to the members of the church at Corinth:

> *"So then, men ought to regard us as servants of Christ and as those entrusted with the secret things of God. Now it is required that those who have been given a trust must prove faithful"* (1Cor 4:1-2).

Members of a local congregation are in fact responsible to reach people with the good news of Christ, to produce fruit. When members sit back, hide out in the crowd and expect others to do the work, the system breaks down and the local church becomes ineffective. The primary task of the elder is to equip disciples so they can, in turn, make disciples. A church that focuses exclusively on reaching the lost will fail to accomplish the mission of making disciples!

Finally, one more problem sometimes develops in the elder led model. Ungodly leaders produce ungodly and unproductive congregations. It may surprise you to learn that many churches appear successful simply on the basis of their size and growth of attenders, but are failing to accomplish the mission because people are leaving as fast as new ones are entering, genuine disciples are not being made and caring relationships are not being developed. Scripture provides a form of checks and balances to assure the ongoing integrity of the office of elder. The ordination process, "the laying on of hands," is one such safeguard in which the congregation is recognizing the authority of its elders and agreeing to be obedient to them. It is not a responsibility that should be taken lightly, and it should never be done hastily. This process becomes an important part of the system of God, in order to prevent a congregation from being led by false teachers.[30] Elders have the responsibility to fulfill the duties assigned by Scripture.

When a person not truly following Christ slips into a position of leadership, the influence upon the congregation can be profound. Care must be taken in the recognition of those who serve as elder. When the work of a congregation becomes controlled by an ungodly or sinning elder, everything breaks down, including the checks and balances God put into place within Scripture. Among these, as discussed above, is the responsibility of members to joyfully follow and obey their leaders. This is impossible to do with a person who is functioning in an ungodly manner. This should not be confused with disobedience to Godly leaders; there is a difference. Further, knowledge of Scripture is in itself a form of checks and balance.

An unproductive congregation is often an uninformed one with regard to the message given in God's Word. For this reason, the expository teaching ministry of the elder is of utmost importance and believers must become involved with the Scripture. Failure to accomplish this task will result in a complete breakdown of the mission given by Christ. Paul describes a process by which a sinning elder is to be disciplined (1Tim 5:19-20). In the previous two chapters of 1 Timothy, Paul had outlined the need for holding elders in high esteem and in providing remuneration for them. In chapter 5 Paul gives an important and necessary safeguard to protect elders against false accusations. Though the context is clearly one in which protection is afforded to an elder, it is easy to identify a form of checks and balances afforded to the congregation. Scripture provides specific instructions for both the discipline and removal of a sinning elder and the authority for this vested to the congregation.[31]

The Biblical Reality on Authority:

It is inaccurate to say that a congregation has no authority and elders have all the authority. It is just as inaccurate to say that a congregation has all the authority and an elder has none. In reality, it is a both/and proposition. The very process of ordination has in it the idea of recognizing and calling elders to serve while committing to support and obey them. But the authority to remove a sinning or ungodly elder is clearly given to the congregation. Ultimately it is Scripture itself that provides the guidelines for authority and obedience.

The presumption is that Scripture is being adequately taught to members and that this teaching is changing lives. An understanding of Scripture goes beyond knowing what it says. Many people can tell you what the Bible says, but some of these do not have a clue what it means. Teaching elders are responsible to see that their flock is well informed about the knowledge and application of Scripture. Their job is made far easier when the people themselves are dedicated to the hard work of study. Ungodly leaders with uninformed congregations lose the system of checks and balances afforded by Scripture and become poor examples of a group of people calling themselves Christians. Remember that a disciple is first and foremost a person who is dedicated to learning God's Word so they can obey all that Christ commanded.

The Logical Conclusion: Elder Led Congregational Government is the Norm

I have attempted to show you the difference between "Congregational" and "Elder Led" models. The Bible supports a balanced view between them. It is neither elder rule nor congregational rule, but rather something in between. Though a variety of structures exist in church government, they can be broken down into five levels, ranging from extreme congregationalism to extreme elder rule. I believe the Bible teaches a balance between them, in which members and elders cooperate, support, and serve one another. This range is represented in the following table.[32] A brief description of each level follows the table. The middle one is probably the most Biblical approach to government within the church.

As you reflect on these five levels of government, ask yourself "Which one are we? Do we need to make a change?"

TABLE 1: Balancing between the extremes

Extreme Congregational Rule	Strong Congregational Rule	Balanced Elder Led Ministry	Strong Elder Rule	Extreme Elder Rule
No Leaders No Followers	Some Leaders Poor Followers	Shepherds Followers	Strong Leader Some Follower	Extreme Lead Only Follow

Extreme Congregational Rule

No leadership, no followship, and control is vested in the "collective everyone"

Ultimate authority is in the collective will of voting members. No one leads and no one follows. Decisions are made by committees. An election process provides for the selection of leaders, but they are never given the authority to actually lead. Decisions made by elected leaders are constantly questioned and criticized. The church flounders for direction because agreement is never reached on a clearly stated mission and vision, resulting in unclear goals and direction. Members and leaders alike become frustrated with the entire process and with their church. The future becomes uncertain. The environment is often uncomfortable and unpredictable. Members may be unwilling to invite people to attend church with them. The result is an inward focus on ministry to membership only, ignoring people within the community who need to find out about the good news of Christ. The mission and purpose of the church, as provided by Christ, is lost. Dysfunctional relationships cause a downward spiral toward ever increasing ineffectiveness as people exert their authority over their leaders.

Strong Congregational Rule

Some leadership is allowed but the congregation must approve everything

The authority is still the collective will of voting members but there is at least some recognition of leadership. Members remain reluctant to submit to and obey their leaders, resulting in poor followship and minimal leadership. Congregations exhibit distrust of leaders, giving them a feeling of uncertainty and confusion and resulting in a lower commitment. Leaders become maintainers of "the status quo" and go through the motions of leading, doing their best not to rock the congregational boat. The church is not driven by vision. Purpose is lost in a sea of tasks that leaders are expected to complete in order to maintain things as they are. Elders (if any are elected) function more like deacons than elders. Deacons may be selected and formed into a governing body representing the authority of the congregation, with authority over that of elder/pastor. The people feel uncomfortable and reluctant to serve in leadership, causing actual leaders to be selected from among a pool of people who volunteer because no one else will do the job. Conflict exists in roles, values, and mission because everyone has a different idea about what they are supposed to do. Elders who try to implement needed changes in order to accomplish the mission become discouraged and are kept from leading.

Balanced Elder Led Ministry

Elders provide strong leadership, balanced by strong teamwork with the congregation and each other.

Elders are recognized, called, and affirmed by the congregation. There is strong leadership and strong followship. Trust exists, resulting in obedience and submission to leaders and caring service by everyone. The congregation encourages and empowers the elders to lead and to make most decisions. Elders, in turn, communicate these decisions to the congregation, keeping them informed and focused on the mission. Ideas and service from members are highly valued and encouraged. The Word of God is read, explained, and applied in a way that changes lives. Elders also communicate vision, mission, purpose and strategy to appointed leaders and the congregation, allowing all to work cooperatively to accomplish the mission. Regular visiting, prayer, and communication takes place among believers, which consist of appointed leaders and members under the authority of the elders. The focus is God, loving Him and each other, which results in an effective ministry that reaches outward into the community. Members of the congregation are encouraged, taught, and shepherded. Leaders have a joy in serving. The church tends to be healthy, and the result is growth of new believers and stronger, more obedient, disciples. In other words, caring teamwork.

Strong Elder Rule

Some decisions are made by congregation as presented by elders.

Strong elder leadership occurs, but only some followship and limited obedience. Leaders make most decisions for the congregation. In many cases, leaders seek their own desires or what they perceive as important without consideration of the feelings or needs of the congregation or their staff. The congregation develops a sense that their opinion and input are not really desired. Leadership fails to release ministry to the congregation. Creativity and collaboration are stifled. Leaders function more as controllers than as coaches or guides. Teamwork is significantly reduced because communication between leaders and members is weak. Ministry is ineffective. Leaders suffer from burnout. Members show up and do the daily stuff of church without being involved in a dynamic ministry.

Extreme Elder Rule

Strong leadership, only followers. Elders decide everything and direct everyone.

Virtually all decisions are made and controlled by elders or a pastoral staff who rule over everything, including selections to various church positions, staff appointments and elections. There exists extremely strong leadership and complete followship. People either get on the bus and do what they are told or encouraged to get out. Decisions are made for the whole church by consensus among the elders, or by the elder with the strongest will, without regard for the opinions or needs of other leaders, employees or congregation. The congregation is seen and treated as followers only. Members of the congregation will either follow the leaders or flee the church. There is no team spirit or shared creativity because there is no team. Leadership is self-perpetuating because the elders choose who will also serve as elders. Over time, expectations for "production" become more important than teamwork or real ministry. This results in a loss of Biblical vision and mission is lost. Growth may be robust in the early stages of this church but will eventually falter because of the lack of genuine discipleship.

How does scripture measure success?

The Scripture measures success by the quality of the relationships that exist between genuine Disciples of Christ. It is quite possible for a church to produce high numbers of people in attendance while failing to achieve the true mission of the church. Elders, who fail to connect people on a path that leads them into a change of thinking and living, who fail to achieve an increase in quality mentoring relationships coupled with obedience to Scripture, will eventually cause a collapse of ministry.

I have observed a church whose senior staff was so focused on producing numbers that they actually failed to care for the people who were trying to achieve the mission. There was virtually no coaching or mentoring. Turnover of staff and pastors was extremely high and the atmosphere stressful. The way in which believers were treated can only be described as harsh, even ruthless. This is not an example of the church as described in Acts Chapter 2, where I make note that it was God who added to their number daily. The emphasis in scripture is in how believers live with and love and encourage each other while being dedicated to the teaching of the Word. The result of living together in a Scriptural way will result in an increase which comes from God. Real growth does not come from some process we follow. Growth comes from a culture that emphasizes the development of people, not on the attraction of attenders. One fuels the other.

When the people of the church do their part to live together for Christ, God can be counted on to do His part. And, growth in maturity and numbers, love and discipleship will be the result.

CHAPTER 3

Huckleberry Finn was conversing with Mary Jane, the red-headed daughter of Peter Wilks. Huck told her that in the church of the Reverend Harvey Wilks, her uncle from Sheffield, there were "no less than 17 clergy." But, he added, "they don't all of 'em preach the same day—only one of 'em." "Well, then," asked Mary Jane, "what does the rest of 'em do." "Oh, nothin much," said Huck. "They loll around, pass the plate, and one thing or another. But mainly they don't do nothin." "Well then, what are they for?" asked Mary Jane in astonishment, to which Huck replied, "Why, they are for style. Don't you know nothin?"[33]

-Mark Twain

Defining the Norm for an Elder

Today's evangelical church is having difficulty defining the role of its leaders. Just what are elders, and what do they do? Against a backdrop of confusion, Biblical error, and even malaise about the ministry of elder, the apostle Paul provides some valuable insight in his valedictory address. We find it in Acts, chapter 20. Here, we learn through observation that an elder is both an overseer and a shepherd, responsible for guiding and ruling the flock.[34] Some churches call them elders or pastors. Some call them overseers or bishops or shepherds. In this passage, while Paul was in the town of Miletus, he summoned the "elders" of the church to attend a meeting (verse 17). During the meeting, Paul said to them,

> *"Keep watch over yourselves and all the flock of which the Holy Spirit has made you* ***overseers****. Be* ***shepherds*** *of the church of God, which he bought with his own blood."* (emphasis mine, Acts 20:28)

Here Scripture clearly uses the terms elder, overseer, and shepherd to refer to the same persons-- those who are responsible for the church of God. The word for elder is sometimes translated presbyter, and overseer translated as bishop, and shepherd as pastor. The terms are interchangeable for the same person. No matter what term, or combination of terms, you use in your church, realize that the position has existed since ancient times.

Old Testament Elder

The Apostles had been given authority under Christ to be the overseers of His church. But these apostles were not destined to live forever. Consequently, they passed on and entrusted the ministry of teaching and rule, called "oversight," to elders. The elders were not appointed as a result of some specific event in the life of the New Testament church, as may be the case with deacons. In fact, Scripture never really tells when the very first elders became set apart or why. Their role and function existed long before the New Testament period, and they were a natural and logical choice for the management of the church of God. In fact, it appears the office of elder belonged to and existed in the government of the church from the very earliest of times.[35]

Elders originated in the most ancient patriarchal period when the people of Israel were scattered across the land in the form of various tribes. In all levels of the Old Testament tradition we find the existence of elders. It is very interesting to note that in the first Hebrew to Greek translation, called the LXX, the word (זְקֵנִי) *zaqen* is translated πρεσβύτερος [36] (pronounced presbuteros), meaning elders. We find the same word throughout the New Testament translated elders. In its singular form the word appears in the Old Testament only ten times, and in each case it refers simply to someone who is old or older. The remaining occurrences are plural, and it is in the plural form that we find the word with the meaning of some office of authority. The first Scriptural appearance of the word in a form used to mean leader, manager, or person with authority is in Genesis 50:7. In this passage (see KJV or NASB) we find the elders of Pharaoh's household attending the funeral of Joseph's father. In this case, they were the managers of Pharaoh's affairs, and Joseph was the highest ranking member!

The word is found with the meaning "one having authority," at least sixty-two times out of 206 occurrences within the Old Testament.[37] There really is no doubt that we find many passages in context where the word elder has the meaning of a leader or manager with some degree of authority. From ancient history and continuing into New Testament times the word often conveys the meaning of oversight authority. As I said before, context is the most important thing when you study the Bible and interpret the meaning of the words you read.

Roles and Duties during Old Testament Times

Elders were the chiefs, the tribal leaders, governors, managers, and even judges. It was the norm in ancient Hebrew society to hear, respect, honor, follow and obey elders. Hebrew people used the term regularly from the earliest patriarchal times to refer to leadership or ruling and oversight. It was also used and recognized by the Moabites, Midianites, and Gibeonites for tribal leaders. Historical records show the elder had become an institution or office of government among the Hittites and the Babylonians from the time of Hammurabi forward. Military commanders were frequently combined with elders to form a governing body. In Scripture, elders who occupied a position of authority gathered at the gate of a city and performed a number of functions as would be expected in a ruling office (Deut 21:19; 22:15, Prov 31:23). These verses are not painting a picture of some group of old codgers hanging out at the city gate to gossip about the coming and going of people. No, they were the ruling elders. Among other functions, they served as judges who tried cases of murder, presided over and settled disputes between individuals, and ratified property transactions.

The Old Testament elder had become an official "office" long before the Exodus, as evidenced in both Scripture and ancient historical documents. Later, in response to a need for a governing body to assist Moses in managing the people (Num 11:16-25), the elder in Israel became both a spiritual office and a position of honor.[38] It is here, in the selection of seventy elders from among the people, that a specific office of government is created, and elders occupied the office. Their role continued to the time of Christ.

The Elders' Role at the Time of Christ

By the time of the New Testament, the Jews had come to accept a system of government in which the elder played a prominent leadership role. The Old Testament cultural idea about an elder was carried over to the New Testament and is in fact a valid foundation for a modern understanding of an elder.[39] In effect, eldership had become institutionalized in the Sanhedrin while councils of elders governed the synagogues. The council of Christian elders first mentioned in Acts 11:30 as receiving gifts for the Jerusalem poor appears on the scene as naturally as did the council of elders to whom Moses was sent long before (Exodus 3:16).[40] At the founding of the New Testament Church, Christ brought together a fellowship based on a structure that was already in place. He did not change the form of government. His fellowship was constructed of men of his own choosing who were accustomed to the mode of government that had prevailed among the Israelites from very early times.

> The office of elder "continued, in substance, what it had been hitherto under the Jewish synagogue system in its best days, with suitable modifications and developments in accordance with the free spirit of the Gospel and the providential circumstances in which the Christian congregations found themselves placed. This presumption is confirmed by all the evidence, direct and indirect, bearing upon the point in the New Testament documents which belong to this period of history."[41]

After the death and resurrection of Christ, authority to lead was given to the apostles. In turn, they began the process of building the church. In virtually every instance in which a community of believers had been developed beyond the missionary stage, the apostles selected and appointed elders, and then worked side by side with them. Though they were second in authority to the apostles, they were destined to become the highest permanent officers in the New Testament church after the apostles passed on. For example, we find the Apostle Paul meeting with the elders of the Jerusalem church in order to share with them the fruits of his missionary travels (Acts 21:15-26). With the death of John, presumably the last apostle to die, Scripture does not seek to continue the office of apostle. The position simply disappears with the death of John. However, this is not the case with the position of elder. Scripture most certainly intended for this position to continue as an office of authority as part of God's system of government.[42]

New Testament Elder

The New Testament takes great pains to specify the particular character attributes that qualify a person to occupy this office (1 Tim 3:1-7, for example). It is important to note that the question of elders, their authority, their function, and the kind of person qualified for the position were not left to chance.

The Apostle Paul, perhaps the greatest missionary who ever lived, appointed elders to a position of leadership in every church he founded. Once a local body had been formed and Paul was ready to move on, a system of government led by elders became the norm. This consistent practice provides compelling evidence that the Gentile churches were to be governed by a system similar to that used among the Jews for centuries. What changed in the New Testament was the emphasis on the character qualifications of a person aspiring to be an elder.

Roles and Duties during New Testament Times

The New Testament elder continued as a respected and honored leader, much the same as the elder of the Old Testament Israelites and synagogue system of the Jews. The accepted lines of authority were not changed. In fact, the concept of elder authority to rule or lead is as true and meaningful to the church today as it was 2000 years ago.[43] At the same time, the New Testament view of elder was more clearly defined in order to make the position one that would bring glory and honor to Christ while achieving the fivefold mission we have already discussed. Though the authority of the position was not diminished in the New Testament, the character and function of the elder most certainly became the focus of Scripture. Further, there appears a greater flexibility in order to accommodate the need to respond to rapid change as the church grew. This flexibility became of utmost importance in order for the early church to survive and flourish. It is the same today, as our culture is in a state of continual change and attack by secular thinking.

> The ministry of rule, like other auxiliary ministries in the church, is free to develop its office according to the needs of the times. In the actual life of the fellowship, therefore, divergent modes of government may emerge.[44]

However, this flexibility for different modes of government presumes the existence of presiding elder or elders, depending on circumstances. The purpose is to allow for a fellowship to respond to outside and internal forces, to accommodate pressing current needs. The presumption here is that elders have the flexibility to respond with a ruling authority when decisions need to be made during a pressing or urgent moment. It becomes the duty of an elder (or elders) to find ways to implement needed change without unduly disturbing the members of the flock, as is required by the instruction to be a servant leader.[45] At the same time, elders are free to develop effective (to borrow from modern human resources management) "empowered and self directed work teams" who labor in cooperation with their elders, who continue to provide the focus, training, and management oversight.

The church was going into all the earth to spread the good news. In encountering new cultures and peoples, it would be important to relate to them. Elders would be responsible for guiding the process. When false teaching or doctrine infiltrated the body, an elder would exercise authority to correct the error. Various developing and differing circumstances required different approaches and responses. There is no difference today. The hope of Scripture is a cooperative team, lived out in caring servant relationships and obedience between leaders and members of the body.

A reading of Acts chapter 2 illustrates the church in action. This chapter describes people who loved God and each other. They were deeply involved in each other's lives through fellowship. They were dedicated students of the Word through the Apostles' teaching. They lived a life of genuine worship as they recognized the worth of God, placing Him first and themselves last. They served each other, sharing what they had as each had need, and were serious about doing ministry together. Evangelism was achieved, not because they were focused on growth, but because the Lord added to their number every day! Too many modern churches have bought into the fantasy that focusing all their efforts on reaching the lost, without an effective plan to disciple them, is the answer to church growth. Oh, that our churches today would look like a true Acts 2 Church. Most do not, though they may call themselves so.

Clearly the hope of a positive functioning evangelical church is rooted in the Biblical assumption that an elder is vested with authority and is expected to lead and manage well.[46] Elders need to be servant leaders who really love God and others, and the congregation should be a people serious about relationships and the Word of God, who willingly cooperate and follow! It should be the same within our churches today. Many churches fail to function like this, and our distaste for the word "submit" at least partially explains this failure. Clearly we have developed a culture that does not like to submit to the authority of someone else. This resistance leads to disobedience, and I believe it is the chief cause of our failure to achieve the results expected of us according to Scripture. Though we apply a negative meaning to the word "submit," the Bible certainly does not. Submission to God the Father is demonstrated by God the Son. Jesus was sent by the Father and submitted to His authority in everything. Therefore, submission must be glorious, not negative! Submission to one another, and especially to leadership, should flow out of our love for each other, just as it flowed out of the love of the Son for the Father. Obedience is part of the very mission statement given by Christ, and submission to leadership is demonstrated by that obedience.

The original sin of Adam and Eve was essentially the sin of refusing to submit to God. The impact was to severely damage their relationship with each other and even creation itself. Submission is not a bad word, but rather a glorious word. In our submission to leaders and one another, we demonstrate to the world a life lived with God as the highest worth (Worship!). If your emotional response to the word is negative, you should pray and reflect on your relationship with Christ. This is especially true of the senior leaders of a church who should learn to listen to and respect the mature people God has guided to them for achieving the work of ministry.

The New Testament Elder Adapted to Change

Over time, the role of an elder became more clearly defined by Scripture itself. As the church changed, adapted, and grew, a variety of circumstances arose that had to be addressed. As a result, flexibility became a necessary ingredient in order for the church to respond to changing circumstances.[47]

First, Scripture does not provide a set number of elders. Thus there is flexibility to have one or more. One of the elder's primary responsibilities is to act as shepherd (pastor). Christ, "the Good Shepherd," serves as the model for elders to emulate. This model implies a close, personal and caring relationship between elder and people. As the church grows, the number of elders required would also grow. In a small house church, one elder may be sufficient. Larger churches need multiple elders. As the need presented itself, elders were able to add to their own number and even create subordinate offices (such as the office of deacon) that were needed for a more harmonious body. As the number of tasks increased, the elders needed more help in order to free them for the work of prayer, ministry, teaching, and management (rule).

The way in which the elders functioned among the body changed as the church grew. At first, they functioned as a self-acting body. Over time, elders apparently began making decisions "with the concurrence" of the congregation. A sort of harmony and teamwork developed between them. At all times the elder is responsible for leading and guiding, but, as the church grew in size and maturity, the people became more involved in the ministry. Clear lines of communication were established as elders explained certain problems and gave direction, and the congregation responded by working with them to accomplish tasks and objectives. Acts 6 and 15 are good examples of this developing teamwork. These passages, taken in context, show the congregation "approving or agreeing with" the elders' direction and decisions. This approval is not the same as a congregational vote, as those who argue for "extreme congregational rule" suggest. In these passages, elders are communicating needs and giving direction, and the congregation is "concurring," "obeying," and "cooperating." The raised hand signifies agreement, not a vote. But just what is an elder? How do we define the person and the job?

Who or What is an Elder?

Elder – Pastor – Overseer: Same thing!

These three words are used in Scripture to describe the same person. In this book I have used elder. It does not matter if you choose one of the other words, or use all of them depending on context. The material I discuss here is only a small part of the available material on the topic. What I have shared so far should be sufficient to establish the fact that elders occupied a position of authority from earliest Biblical history and continuing into the New Testament church. If you still hold doubts, please study the books listed in the Annotated Bibliography and the word studies found in the Appendix. I have attempted to be thorough in citing quality references and works for you. Now I would like to focus on understanding who the elder is and especially what the job entails. To do so we will start with a job description and then pursue a definition by analyzing the words used in Scripture to describe elders.

An Elder's Job Description

The key element of an elder's "job description" can be found in Scripture:

> *"It was he who gave some to be apostles, some to be prophets, some to be evangelists,* ***and some to be pastors and teachers, to prepare God's people for works of service*** (emphasis mine), *so that the body of Christ may be built up until we all reach unity in the faith and in the knowledge of the Son of God and become mature, attaining to the whole measure of the fullness of Christ"* (Eph 4:11-13).

I have often heard this passage referred to as a "Five Fold Ministry," referring to apostles, prophets, evangelists, pastors, and teachers as five separate ministries. This understanding is flawed because of an error in interpreting Greek grammar. It is not a fivefold ministry, but a fourfold ministry. The "pastor and teacher" is one and the same person or group. In the context of this passage, *"to prepare God's people for works of service"* is referring back or pointing to "the pastor and teacher," also known as elder or overseer.

The original Greek here uses the definite article τοὺς (pronounced toos) meaning "the," in a manner linking pastor and teacher as the same person. In the original we find this definite article appearing with each of the four categories of people and ministries being described: "the apostles," "the prophets," "the evangelists," and "the pastors and teachers." If the ministry of teaching had been intended to be separate from the ministry of pastor, the definite article would have appeared before each word, as "the pastors and the teachers." In fact, the scholars who translated the New International Version carefully inserted commas into the text to help us with correct interpretation. Here, the word structure and grammar for "the pastor and teacher" is referring to one person, not two.

Though it is certainly possible to be a teacher without being a pastor, here Scripture links the concept of pastor with that of teacher, which agrees with what we have already learned about the oral tradition of rabbinic learning (Mishnah). The more accurate description of this passage would be a "Four Fold Ministry," in which the pastor and teacher represent the same person. One cannot be a pastor without also being a teacher of God's Word, like the Rabbis of old. In fact, one of the few abilities listed for the pastor is the ability to teach: the apostle Paul said to Timothy,

"Now the overseer... must be able to teach" (1Ti 3:2).

How does one become ready to teach the Word of God?

In Ecclesiastes chapter 10 we find some wise words regarding the work of preparation for doing any job, but especially in doing a job for God. Here the passage begins with contrasting the smell of dead flies in perfume with the little errors we make that outweigh wisdom and honor. A lack of skill and preparation for any work will bring poor results. The solution is found in the verse saying,

> *"if the axe is dull and he does not sharpen its edge, then he must exert more strength. Wisdom has the advantage of giving success"* (NASB Ecclesiastes 10:10).[48]

In other words, take the time to prepare yourself for a task before you begin it. Sharpen your ax before you start cutting trees. Study God's Word before you start teaching it. The pastor and teacher must be prepared to teach accurately in order to lead the flock of God correctly; otherwise everyone will be led astray by a well meaning shepherd who does not know the way or how to manage the process of achieving the mission.

In many New Testament passages the terms pastor, shepherd, overseer, and bishop are interchangeable with elder. The instruction of Scripture to deploy the saints for ministry applies to this person, and the job is impossible unless people are taught, and taught well. The passage describes the duty of an elder, and it is an ongoing primary job description to *"Prepare God's people for works of service."*[49] A people who will not follow, who will not make the hard work of study and learning a priority, cannot be equipped to serve.

Many theologians would argue that the ministries of "apostle" and "prophet" were discontinued in the New Testament church with the deaths of John the Baptist and John the Revelator; perhaps so. God has completed his written revelation to man, and we now have the Bible in our hands. With it we can speak the very words of God. Isn't this the main thing that a prophet did? With the transfer of apostolic authority to elders, we have been given shepherds to follow. Are we not expected to obey them? Of course we are.

But the ministry of evangelist continues for everyone. To evangelize is synonymous with "spreading the Good News," and we have already seen that "evangelism" is an important component of the mission provided by Christ. It is the duty of every believer to *"Go therefore and make disciples...,"* or "evangelize." The duty of the elder is to prepare God's people for the job (help them sharpen their ax) so that together they can accomplish the mission of Christ. The Scripture supports team ministry, not dictatorship.

It is compelling to note that Scripture even tells us how long the elder's duty is expected to continue. The job continues until a specific future event takes place: an event described as a day when the body of Christ has been built up to the point where all are in unity, all believe in Christ and are *mature* in their faith (Ephesians 4:13). That day is not yet here, not by a long shot. So the job of elder continues.

Understanding the Term "Elder"

Elders are still very much needed in our church today. A clear and solid understanding of what exactly an "elder" is becomes important. I have stated several times that key terms are used interchangeably in the New Testament to refer to the elder. I would like to move toward a clearer definition of "elder" by discussing these terms with you.

> For centuries churchmen and theologians have battled over the issue of church government in hope of supporting the kind of church order they advocate. Episcopalians, Presbyterians, and Baptists, for example, hold widely differing views on church government. To some degree their differences stem from the way they understand the Biblical term "elder." Therefore a study of how the term is used in the Scriptures is an important step in understanding church government.[50]

The New Testament uses five important and highly descriptive words to identify and describe an elder. Several of these words are interchangeable and refer to the same person or group of people.[51] In fact, we have already seen the Apostle Paul using the terms *elders, overseers and shepherds* (Acts 20:17, 28) to refer to the same persons. He used the word "elder" as the title referring to them, the word "overseer" as a reference to their authority, and the word "shepherd" to instruct them on how to do their job. In this one section of Scripture Paul gathers the *elders,* calls them *overseers,* and tells them to act like *shepherds.* Paul is not the only one to make this connection.

Peter writes,

> *To the elders among you, I appeal as a fellow elder, a witness of Christ's sufferings and one who also will share in the glory to be revealed: Be shepherds of God's flock that is under your care, serving as overseers--not because you must, but because you are willing, as God wants you to be; not greedy for money, but eager to serve; (1Pe 5:1-2).*

It is compelling to see that Peter refers to himself as a fellow elder. It is noteworthy that he used the word elder and not the word priest. One of the greatest apostles here makes a clear correlation between his oversight authority as an elder and that of his fellow elders, instructing them to serve as "overseers." Functioning as a "shepherd" then becomes the norm and to function as a shepherd the elder should work diligently at conforming to the image of Christ in order to set a proper example. The great teacher Augustine discusses the oversight authority of an elder along with the duty to act like a servant leader who shepherds the flock of God. He described the elders' diligence to conform to the life of a servant leader as "self watch" and placed great importance on this for an elder to be effective in the role.[52]

Two additional words are clearly associated with those who have been put in the position of being an elder: *leader* and *manager.* In Acts 7:10 the word ἡγέομαι (pronounced hegeomai) is translated "ruler" in the New International Version and "governor" in the New American Standard Version. It is the very same word often translated "leader." Acts 7:10 reminds us of the story of Joseph, describing how he was made the "ruler or leader or governor'" over all the land of Egypt. This same word is used here in Hebrews:

> *Obey your **leaders** and submit to their authority. They keep watch over you as men who must give an account. Obey them so that their work will be a joy, not a burden, for that would be of no advantage to you.* (emphasis mine *Heb 13:17)*

This word "obey" has become a difficult one for a sinning world, particularly in a culture that does not like to "submit." It is especially difficult for Americans, who want to be in the driver's seat and free to call our own shots, be our own boss, and submit to no one. It is a matter of spiritual maturity to learn how to follow one's leaders by submitting to their authority. Being obedient to our elders causes their work to be a joy as they serve as our shepherds and overseers.

We also find a clear teaching referring to the overseer as a manager. The Bible uses the word οἰκονόμος (pronounced oikonomos) meaning steward or manager in Titus 1:7. In the New American Standard Bible, speaking of the overseer we are told he must be "above reproach as God's **Steward**." The NIV translates the word "entrusted with God's work."

We thus find five important words used in the New Testament that can be used to arrive at a clearer definition: elder (presbyter), overseer (bishop), pastor (shepherd), leader (governor/ruler) and steward (manager). So you will have no doubt of the claims I am making, let's consider each word in more detail.[53]

Definitions and Word Study

Elder

Elder comes to us from the Greek word πρεσβύτερος (pronounced presbuteros) that was translated into Greek from the Old Testament Hebrew word זְקֵנֵי - zaqen (pronounced Zaw-Kane). It is the word translated elder or presbyter and the word from which we get "presbytery." It has been in existence from the earliest of times, found both in the Bible and in ancient literature. Throughout the Old Testament and continuing into the New Testament, elders have occupied an office of authority and rule. The word appears in its plural form two hundred and six times in the Old Testament, with sixty-two of these occurrences conveying the idea of one having authority over others, as in tribal or governing authority.[54] It appears seventy-seven times in the New Testament, with the greatest concentration found in the Book of Acts. When taken in context the word can convey the following meanings: "ambassador for Christ," "older man or woman," "a manager or steward," "a council of managers," and "as a member of a ruling body of elders over a local church."

For our purposes, the elders we are discussing are in a position of authority, occupying a church office that expects members to obey as they would an apostle and acting as ambassadors for Christ on behalf of the body of Christ.[55] They have been given the responsibility to guide the church like a senator. An interesting correlation is found in ancient literature, where the word is used to describe the helmsman or captain of a ship, and it came to be associated with one who would steer a "ship of state."[56] There is no greater human authority on earth than a captain of a ship at sea. The term seems to refer more to the authority of an office such as "an office of government." A number of passages, like Matthew 15:2 and Mark 7:3-5, clearly present the elder as a person who occupies a place of dignity and authority, having been duly appointed within a community as a leader.[57] However, one should note that these particular elders were not functioning in a manner consistent with the teaching of Christ. My point is to help you note the position of elder as accepted by the people at the time. The position has not changed: the character and duties have changed.

When the word appears as a noun, it typically conveys a meaning consistent with the idea of "an office." As a verb, the word "elder" conveys the meaning "the exercise of authority." As an adjective, it describes the person to whom the "authority of the office" has been given. In the context of referring to those who are given the authority to oversee the church, the word typically appears as a noun. In other passages, elders are also referred to and called overseers.

Overseer - Bishop

Overseer comes to us from the Greek word ἐπίσκοπος (pronounced episkopos) that was translated from the Old Testament Hebrew word הִפְקִיד (pronounced Paw-Kad). It is the same word translated as bishop and was adopted as part of a title in the Episcopal Church, which uses a system with bishops, similar to that in the Roman Catholic Church. In the vast majority of cases where it is used, the word refers to the holder of an office of authority. The word elder describes the office, whereas overseer refers to the person who occupies it. The word occurs eleven times in the New Testament. Each occurrence discusses the holder of an office of authority, the office of bishop or overseer. The overseer is a "guardian," who has the job to "see after," or oversee, and take care of the New Testament Church. In a distinctly Christian sense, the word refers to the activity of church officials who are called overseers or bishops.[58]

The term translated as bishop or overseer becomes synonymous with elder or presbyter, as well as pastor or shepherd. From the earliest times of the Christian church, the word described a person who occupies an office having the duties of oversight and judgment.[59] It is a position one can aspire to (1Ti 3:1), and a worthy aspiration it is. The purpose for having this person in the office is to ensure that the organized church has continuity after the missionary's job is done and an organized body of believers has been formed.[60] The person in this office also makes sure that the body of believers is served, guarded, and shepherded, and leads the church in the fulfillment of its fivefold purpose. A list of character qualifications describes the holder of this position.

When applied to the elder, the term "oversee" has the same sense as the "master of a house," "a ship's captain," or "a merchant in charge of various goods." The word undoubtedly refers to the work of supervision and control. Christ himself is called overseer (1Peter 2:25), and the word serves to strengthen the authority of the shepherd or pastor of the flock of God.[61]

The duties of the overseer are to manage, oversee, watch over, care for, supervise, lead, teach, preach and rule. In short, the position is one of servant leadership, and it is only logical to conclude that the flock is expected to follow those holding this position. In this word, especially in its adjective or descriptive form, we gain understanding about the kind of person, especially in regard to their character, who would occupy the office of elder. In the word elder we often find a noun that tells us about the office of authority under Christ. In the word overseer we often find an adjective that describes what qualifies a person to occupy the office. You can readily identify a church who understands the role of an overseer by looking at the process they follow to call one to serve in the office of elder.

> Regarding the pastoral call process; rarely does a questionnaire deal with character traits. Despite that we call ourselves 'evangelicals' and claim to be Biblical in our approach, we fall short of the Biblical standard in this matter. Although the Bible often states the kinds of things that elders, pastors, or overseers do, nowhere does it specify the talents we may expect of them. Nowhere does it state that they must be exceptional managers, visitors, pulpiteers, or teachers. Although they need those qualities to perform their duties, the Bible's major emphasis is in an entirely different direction; instead of insisting on how well a person is able to perform certain functions, it focuses instead on what kind of a person he is.[62]

The elder is an overseer (bishop) and also a pastor (shepherd). We have seen the meaning of elder in the noun form, describing the office itself. We have seen the meaning of overseer in the adjective form, describing the duties and character qualifications of the person who would serve. Finally, we find the verb describing how they are expected to function. The verb or action word is pastor or shepherd.

Pastor – Shepherd

Pastor or shepherd comes to us from the Greek word ποιμήν (pronounced poimane) translated from the Old Testament Hebrew word רָעֶה (pronounced Raw-Aw). The word is translated interchangeably as both pastor and shepherd. It appears in the New Testament thirty-nine times in eleven books, mostly in the Gospels. For those who claim that the word elder only refers to a person who is older, would they also say that the word shepherd only refers to the one who cares for a flock of sheep? Of course not: in context, the verb form of the word describes the person who leads, guides, and rules[63] the flock of God as it travels down the road of discipleship. In fact, from linking "to tend as a shepherd" to "pastoring the flock," we readily arrive at the idea of governing and guiding.[64]

This word appears mostly as a verb when referring to the pastor or elder of the church. It appears as a noun especially when it is referring to Jesus Christ, the Great Shepherd who sets the example for all to follow. It is in His example as a servant to others that we find the expectation of how an elder is supposed to function, namely as a pastor or shepherd. Christian elders were exhorted not to be self seeking masters over the community, but rather examples of service to it.[65] Love God and love others, right? God first, me last is what God expects of us, and it is the elders who are to show us how, by demonstrating their "servant leadership" to us as we learn to follow their example.

Though the culture of Jesus' day had a negative view of shepherds in their society, the New Testament had a distinctly positive one. Jesus did not hesitate to use the term to describe God. Only once in the New Testament is the word used specifically of congregational leaders who are called shepherds, translated "pastors" in Ephesians 4:11. As described previously, the absence of the Greek article before the word teacher shows clearly that pastors and teachers, also called shepherds, form a single group of people. They are responsible to minister to the entire congregation: to lead, guide and equip the members for the mission. They are the leaders of the local church and responsible in part to combat against heresy and incorrect teaching, to seek the lost, and to be an example to the flock so they will learn how to be a disciple of Christ.[66]

The shepherd cares for the congregation, providing leadership [command], protection, instruction, guidance, oversight, and rule. The elder occupies an office and should receive honor. Elders should place the needs of the flock above their own and should never take on the duties of shepherd for personal gain. In this sense, shepherds should have the character attributes that make them worthy of the calling. They are servants of Christ who are to set an example for the congregation to follow. The shepherd (pastor) leads people in "The Way of Christ." In this word we have a verb describing what the pastor does while serving as an overseer, occupying the office of elder. The word "pastor" is the verb by which we can come to a better understanding of what it means to "shepherd the flock of God" as found in 1 Peter 5:1-4.[67]

As I said, the words are used interchangeably to refer to the same group of people. An elder is an overseer (bishop) and also a pastor (shepherd). We can glean an even better understanding when we consider how the word "leader" is used in connection with the position.

Leader – Governor - Ruler

Leader comes to us from the Greek word ἡγεμόνοις (pronounced heygemonois) translated from the Old Testament Hebrew word נָגִיד (pronounced Naw-Gheed). This word is used to convey the meaning of governing and ruling. It was used in the first Greek translation of the Old Testament with this meaning. It appears in the New Testament twenty-four times, and each time refers to a ruler, ruling body, or governor with the authority to lead. In general, the word is used of one having the authority to direct affairs as within an office of management.[68]

The New Testament church had rules in place for the purpose of guiding the behavior of Christian believers. These behavioral patterns are defined within the context of a Christian household that included various classes of people: husbands and wives, parents and children, and masters and slaves. Christians were addressed according to their station in life, especially within the household. The key thought in the New Testament regarding behavior within God's household is found in the terms "obedience" and "submission." The reason for this is because such attitudes are the best way to demonstrate subordination to the Lordship of Christ. It is within this context that the term "leaders" is used to convey the instruction for the members of God's house to be obedient. Being obedient to those who have been placed in authority is both a representation of Christian maturity and a demonstration of obedience to Christ.[69]

When the writer of Hebrews (13:17) admonished the people to obey their leaders it was in the context of "those who were placed in authority over you," namely overseers (or pastors or elders, if you prefer). The community of believers is obviously divided into two groups: those who lead and those who are led. The founders of the Christian community after Christ are listed among those leaders and serve as examples to their flock.[70]

Certain people within the Christian community are called to a position of authority and asked to lead the members of the community. The authority of the original founders has been passed on to them. This word was clearly understood by original readers to mean "governor or ruler." These leaders (elders/overseers/pastors) are holders of an office, as in an office of government. This calling should not be confused with a "democracy," for these leaders are responsible primarily to God and will be held accountable by Him for their actions. Scripture associates them with this word "ruler," and they are expected to fulfill the duties of leading and ruling the congregation.

Within the context of the Greek use of the word, members of a congregation are expected to obey their leaders just as they would be expected to obey Christ Himself, a man who would wash your feet for you. In fact, in that time the word was used also of a military captain or governor who rightly expected obedience (there is that word we don't like again) from their subordinates. A system of government is certainly the expectation in Scripture. Submission, without grumbling but with joy, to the authority of those who occupy leadership positions is a part of Christian piety and a demonstration of obedience to Christ. Scripture also presumes an elder who functions as a servant leader. I have described one of the five purposes of Christ for the church as "discipleship." This component of the mission comes from the words "teach them to obey." Obedience is the mark of a disciple.

Finally, understand that one who is placed in authority over others also has the duty of oversight and should strive to manage well. The elder is also referred to in the context of being a manager of God's House. We find the word often translated as "steward," which is the last word we will consider in this word study.

Steward – Manager - Administrator

Steward comes to us from the Greek word οἰκονόμον (oikonomon). The word is commonly used in the New Testament to refer to a manager of some responsibility and also to the authority that goes with it. Literally it means "manager of a household." A steward is trusted to manage the affairs and possessions that belong to someone else. The word describes one who manages the master's property and is ultimately accountable to Him.[71] The implication for an elder should be obvious.

In the New Testament, "steward" comes to rest on the idea of having responsibility to manage the affairs of God on behalf of His household and to share the Gospel message. With stewardship comes the responsibility of management and the duty to accomplish the task of administration. All Christians are called to be "stewards" (managers) of the "mystery of God" (1Cor 4:1-2) as they do the work of evangelism. But when the word is linked with overseer or bishop (most notably in Tit 1:7), it simply provides further understanding of the expectation God has for a person occupying the position within His organizational plan. Here Scripture states clearly that the overseer is to be above reproach as God's steward, one who is entrusted to do the work of God – His chosen manager.

Remember, however, that the elder serves as an overseer but acts like a pastor. The expectation is for this person to function as a servant leader, the way Christ taught them to serve. The elder is called to be the shepherd of God's flock. This is most certainly a position of leadership with the duty to manage. Throughout the Old Testament and carried right through in the New Testament, the elder is clearly the chosen instrument by which the church is to be led.[72] Scripture makes clear the kind of leader that God has in mind for this job, and it has nothing to do with acting like a dictator who "lords it over" the people. An elder should be loving, not haughty; humble, not superior; serving, not overbearing. Elders are to lead from in front of the people, setting an example for them to follow, inviting them to do so.[73] Patience and mentoring, care and coaching, serving and teaching should be the hallmark of one who would be a leader in the house of our God.

An Elder Defined

In summary then, a definition for an elder can be stated as follows:

> "A person with the character traits of a servant leader who manages and governs by overseeing the affairs of the church of God, teaching the word of God in order to help others learn how to follow and obey Christ, fostering relationships and teamwork

while acting with the same authority as a "captain of a ship at sea," who is responsible for leading the body of Christ on a path of discipleship."

What it Means to Lead

Servant leadership is not non-leadership. On the contrary, servant leaders lead, but with a style not reflective of the popular culture. Jesus instructed his followers to walk away from prevailing Gentile and Jewish models of prideful leadership, where dominance (lording it over) coercion, titles, and public recognition were the goals. *"Not so with you,"* Jesus explained in Matthew 20:26.[74]

It is a primary responsibility of the elder to provide Biblical leadership. Leadership under the Biblical model is influenced by the character attributes described within its pages. Servant leaders are sure of their position with God and know they are valued. Servant leaders experience joy when they find a way to provide encouragement to their members and teams. They are not in search of credit or recognition for the things that they do and they exhibit patience with people who may be in need of coaching. Relationships with people are very important to the servant leader. They have no wish to manipulate or control people's actions. Rather, they desire to influence them toward discipleship through teaching, coaching, mentoring, building relationships, setting examples, and providing encouragement.

In his second letter to Timothy, Paul gives a compelling reason why a trained leader, a disciple, should be convinced of his or her faith. He said, *"But as for you, continue in what you have learned and become convinced of,* ***because you know those from whom you learned it"*** (2 Timothy 3:14 emphasis mine). What are we convincing people of as we are observed by them? Those of us in leadership should be demonstrating a faith that is convincing to others. Nowhere will this be truer than in our management of the people who work with and for us. Leadership that creates friction and division and stress and turnover is not servant leadership that values the development of people toward Christ likeness. Such leadership demonstrates a ruthless corporate culture rather than a loving Christian one. When I see division, stress and turnover among Christians, especially among leaders and staff, it makes me wonder if this Christian life is just another false religion. Christian leaders, who mentor, forgive, encourage and guide in patient relationships; who move into the world with that kind of love become a very convincing proof that Christianity is indeed true! Our flock will be convinced of their faith because they know us and follow our example. Or will they? After all we can expect the people who follow us to achieve the same result we produce ourselves, and the Bible says that a bad tree cannot produce good fruit (Matthew 7:18).

Servant leaders do not seek out opportunities to demonstrate authority or elevate themselves to lofty positions higher than the people they lead. No, a servant leader is willing to bend down and wash the feet of those being served and this should be especially true for the people who are called to work alongside them. The office has an assumed authority, but servant leaders base their authority more on their character, Scripture, and its job description than in the office they hold or in their own self confidence or ambition or goals. Jesus used himself as an example of servant leadership, saying that such a servant

> *"will not quarrel or cry out; no one will hear his voice in the streets. A bruised reed he will not break, and a smoldering wick he will not snuff out"* (Mat 20:19-20).[75]

CHAPTER 4

If I had to define my task as a pastor and elder, I would sum it up simply by saying this: "Win, teach, train, send." We don't have to work hard to determine what we're supposed to do. We are to teach the Word of God. Why? To win people to Christ. Why? So they can grow in the faith. Why? So they can be trained to win people to Christ. Then we send them out to do that very thing![76]

- John MacArthur

What an Elder Does

In Evangelical churches you seldom hear the term "bishop" or "overseer." A dear friend of mine is a pastor in a church that recently left their former denomination over its move toward liberal theology that was clearly disobedient to the clear teaching of Scripture. His church is standing firm on God's Word and their new national organization defines a "bishop" as a "pastor of pastors." I like this way of clarifying a role and making terms clear. Often you find churches who call people to serve as an elder, but then fail to define the role clearly.

Virtually every church has a pastor or team of pastors, and many have elders too. The terms we use today have come to mean something different than the original meaning found in Scripture. For the most part, Protestants avoid using the term "overseer/bishop" out of fear that it will sound like some form of Roman Catholicism. We use the term "pastor" loosely to describe a person who receives compensation for the job as a full time occupation. Sometimes we use the word "shepherd" or "under-shepherd" or "lay leader" to refer to someone who is a leader of a ministry or small group. We often use the term "elder" for the member of some kind of board without understanding what they are supposed to do, and, more often than not, neither do they! We may delegate oversight to them but fail to recognize their authority or understand their job according to Scripture. Sometimes we use the term "Deacon Board" to describe some governing body acting with the same authority as "elders," or even a higher authority. Confusing and often unBiblical!

This may be the best argument I can make for the Scriptural model that suggests elders are appointed by other elders and recognized by the congregation. It takes one to know one, so to speak. It takes one to train one, too. The congregation can and should be involved in the process of identifying those who demonstrate the character qualifications while functioning among them like a shepherd. At the same time, their ability to recognize the elders among them is limited by the quality of their education and understanding on the subject. Perhaps this book will be of assistance in teaching them. I hope so! Far too often, an elder is nominated by the congregation because they are well liked or perceived to be a "good person." As I have demonstrated so far, the Bible uses these terms as referring to the same group of people. So why is the modern church so confused in its use of terms?

Why so much Confusion?

Generally we find elders called to serve for a term on some sort of a board, apparently with a limited degree of authority within the church. But since we also have pastors in the same church, their roles often become confused. When roles are not clearly defined, often a rift develops between the pastors and elders. One group tries to influence or control the other. Problems often develop. Hardly ever do you hear quality teaching on the subject. Often the elder board has a fixed number of seats, something the Scripture does not suggest. When it comes time to fill a vacant position on the elder board, the members of the congregation are asked to nominate anyone they feel is qualified for it. People who have an agenda to change things lobby members for nomination. Faction groups get behind their chosen candidate. As these folks are installed on the board, confusion and dysfunction become the norm as the people hunker down and get really busy doing all kinds of things that have nothing to do with accomplishing the mission. Everyone looks busy, but to what purpose? Scripture suggests that the people need a vision in order to stay on the path. *Where there is no vision, the people are unrestrained, But happy is he who keeps the law* (NASB Proverbs 29:18).

No wonder we have arrived at such a point of confusion. How often do you find elders doing their best to serve the church by arriving early to set up or take down chairs for a function? Or serve food and help do the dishes with the guys after a meal? Or maybe they get together periodically to pray (an important function) because they just do not have anything else to do. As a result they find ways to be busy at something, anything, to serve. Though there is nothing wrong with doing these things, we will see many of these special kinds of service were eventually delegated to a new office of serving called "deacon." The purpose of setting aside these forms of service was to free the elders for their ministry of prayer and teaching the Word of God: to allow them to fulfill their job description of equipping the saints for works of service.

Who has taught the elders what their job is and how to do it so the work can be effectively passed on to others? Elders have oversight authority and are supposed to shepherd the flock of God. Have they been prepared for the job? Have they learned how to duplicate themselves and train new leaders who understand the importance? Growing churches need more than one elder, though the number is undefined. A church needs as many as it will take to get the job done, and elders should learn to function as a team, following the one who is their leader. I would strongly suggest that if your church is not growing, or has become stuck on a plateau, you should consider how you are doing in this important area. Growth should be measured both in numbers and spiritual maturity. Poor organization and communication coupled with a lack of Biblical vision with regard to structure and job description may be the problem. Your elders and pastors should be working well together, sharing the load in a way that recognizes that they all have the same basic job description. Is there harmony between them in your church? No? Is there high turnover among your staff and pastors? Yes? Hopefully this book will help you solve the problem by providing a solution.

Clearing Things Up

I have prayed for this book to clear the fog from the air and allow for a more Scriptural understanding of the elder. I have no problem with the idea of using the term "elder" to describe a volunteer and the term "pastor" to refer to one who is paid for the job as long as the following conditions are met: their authority as "overseers" is publicly recognized; they act like shepherds, working well together as a team; their job description is understood; and the congregation knows who and what they are. In the modern Evangelical Church a part time or volunteer elder should have the same basic function as a full time paid pastor. They just spend less time doing it, and in most churches do not receive compensation. Obviously, in a church that has grown to a size where one elder/pastor cannot do the job alone, it becomes natural to add to their number. As soon as you do so, you have created a team that needs to be managed and organized with clear lines of authority, yet with cooperation. In the absence of good management, confusion and dysfunction will increase. We often refer to the importance of "mentoring relationships" in church. Nowhere is this so important than for mentoring to exist among pastors and elders who are responsible to "mentor" the flock of God.

I would go so far as to suggest the title "Senior Pastor" may be applicable to the leader of the elder/pastor team. But the management style should be described as a servant leader, coaching as the Scripture is followed while keeping everyone focused on the mission and leading by example. In larger churches, the creation of a new position called "Executive Pastor" seems to be in direct response to the Senior Pastor becoming overwhelmed and needing help with management! An Executive Pastor may serve directly under the Senior Pastor to provide a more effective team through management and oversight. Scripture provides flexibility to allow for adaptation based on the changing needs of a growing church. Just be careful that you don't make the mistake of confusing success as a business manager with success as a pastor.

If careful attention is paid at the beginning (the call process), a church will avoid choosing elders (pastors) who should not have been called. It also helps to keep from delegating elder authority to a person who should not have been given it in the first place. At all levels of church government there is order and obedience because we serve a God of order who expects it. The goal is to achieve the purpose of the church, to accomplish the "vision" through effective organization and management that offers great encouragement to those who serve.

The Bible should always, *always,* be the blueprint to follow. Bylaws and rules should come from the Bible and never have authority over it. We should never point to some other document and say, "We have to do it this way because that is what the by-laws say, sorry." Doing so becomes the means by which people control the church instead of God controlling people. Many churches have installed leaders who are driven by personal agendas and who use the writing of by-laws to achieve their own ends. Beware of allowing your by-laws or other rules or electoral process outside the Bible to become the tool of the powerless to obtain power. Knowledge and application of Scripture would solve practically any problem in the church, with or without "by-laws!" The primary job of teaching was given to the elder so the people could be taught to obey God, not man; so they could be provided with a vision that lights the path of discipleship. Make sure your by-laws are aligned with Scripture and defer to its authority as the final say in all matters.

This issue serves as yet another example of why the overseer must be able to teach. When the flock is left to their own devices and receives no clear guidance and sound teaching, they will stray. When you call people from among them to serve as elders, then those called are often not qualified and have not been properly trained in God's Word, and the straying becomes a stampede. So, please be clear in your use of the terms and how you are applying them in your congregation. Never lose sight of the fact that the Bible uses several terms to refer to the same group of people. It does not matter if you call them elder, pastor, overseer, bishop, shepherd, or some combination of terms as long you clear up the confusion over their meaning. If our goal is to be obedient to His Word, then we should strive to apply it correctly and clear up the misunderstanding and miscommunication in this all important area. Remember the old saying, "A mist in the pulpit makes a fog in the pew."

Now we need to consider what the elders' responsibilities are. We can summarize their many responsibilities into three basic categories:

- Administration (Overseeing)
- Teaching (Preaching)
- Shepherding (Pastoring).

In the following section I will present detailed instructions gleaned from Scripture. I challenge you to identify any specific elder/pastor responsibility in Scripture that does not fall into one of these three main categories. In the next chapter we will consider the organization of an elder team that would allow them to function more effectively and joyfully too. For now, let me review the responsibilities of an elder.

The Elders' Responsibilities

Paul classifies all those to whom ruling authority in the church is given under the general title of "elders." He then points to the special function of teaching and preaching. On the basis of this observation it *may* be possible to make a case for ordination of "pastors" to be responsible for teaching and preaching and "elders" for church administration or a board of some kind. However, if true, such ordination does not confer a superior authority or status of one over the other, at least not from Scripture.[77] It also does not prohibit an elder from participation in the teaching ministry, especially since the ability to teach is a Biblical requirement for the position.

Detailed Instructions from the Word of God

Scripture provides ample instruction on the subject of elders. I have prepared an analysis of nearly fifty references organized in three tables. This listing is not exhaustive, but the work is sufficient to identify the specific duties Scripture would include in the elders' job description. Some of the passages are contained within personal letters of instruction directed specifically to an elder. These passages are clear and instructive. Other passages are making another point but simultaneously describe actions of the elders of the church. We can gain insight by observing what the elders are doing. It's like using your peripheral vision to see something you are not actually looking at. We should do our best to pay attention to the duties expected of the elder and submit to their authority under Christ because Scripture makes their list of duties pretty clear.[78]

From an analysis of Scripture it is possible to describe the elders' duties, categorizing each one into one of the three main areas of responsibility. Perhaps it will help you understand why Scripture tells us that an overseer must be able to teach. Perhaps you can also understand why Scripture provides a job description that identifies one person or group of people to be the *"pastor and teacher"* who is responsible for *"preparing the saints to do the works of service,"* and why it is important to *"obey them."*

I have analyzed the Scripture references in order to describe each of the three primary areas of responsibility, followed by a fairly exhaustive list of duties for each. To be successful at achieving the work given in their job description, the elders administrate, teach and shepherd.

Defining the Three Primary Categories of Responsibility

Administration (Oversight)

Oversight means both the responsibility to manage and the authority to lead. It means managing as a leader and a steward of the house of God, for the purpose of guiding the flock toward achieving the mission. It means understanding what to do and being capable, with the help of Christ, to coordinate the right people to get the work done. It means an ability to delegate jobs to a people who will accept responsibility for them. Do not confuse administration with the idea of task only management. An elder/pastor is responsible primarily for managing people, not things. I have seen some well meaning spiritual gifts inventories define "administration" as task management, even using the term "bean counter" to describe it. Doing repetitive tasks like counting inventory, making budgets, creating spreadsheets, doing accounting, and the like may be very important jobs, but they are not pastoral jobs. For our purposes, administration is referring to the good management of people and turning them loose to get ministry done. This requires leadership, which carries the implication that the flock will follow (obey) as the overseer leads them by example in obedience to Christ. It means having the authority to put people in the game: sending them out to "do works of service" and accomplishing that work with a commitment to excellence out of dedication to Christ;

> *"Whatever you do, work at it with all your heart, as working for the Lord, not for men"* (Colossians 3:23).

TABLE 2: ADMINISTRATION AND OVERSIGHT DUTIES

SCRIPTURE	HOW THIS APPLIES TO ADMINISTRATION AND OVERSIGHT
Acts 6:1-6	Appoint ministry leaders, servers, deacons. Delegate service jobs to others who are qualified to serve in a leadership position, like the deacon. Get help from good people so you can free yourself to focus on the ministry of the Word of God.
Acts 11:30	Take responsibility for financial support intended for the relief of believers.

Acts 14:20	Appoint elders over the flock of God in every church.
Acts 15:1-6	When confusion or disagreement exists, gather the elders together and work it out. Work together.
Acts 15:20-23	Select people from among the congregation to serve alongside and with you. Do your work with the participation of the whole church.
Acts 16:4	After making decisions, communicate them to the members of the church and keep them informed.
1Tim 1:3-5	Bring correction using the Word of God – reprove, rebuke, exhort, encourage. Keep your people on course.
1Tim 1:18-19	Fight for the purposes of God and His divine truth, fight to keep your conscience clean and your faith strong.
1Tim 3:1-13	Select people and appoint them to serve as spiritual leaders within the church. Do this carefully. Choose those who are qualified according to demonstrated gifts, godliness and virtue.
1Tim 4:7-11	Pay attention to manage yourself. "Self watch." Stay attentive to your own spiritual growth; be disciplined for the purpose of godliness.
1Tim 5:3-16	Direct the people to provide for widows, orphans, and families, and make sure the needs are communicated and see that instructions to provide for one another are carried out by the people.
1Tim 5:17-21	Give honor to those who serve as fellow elders, especially those who work hard at preaching and teaching. Encourage them and see they are provided for.
1Tim 5:22-23	Be careful and attentive to the ordination process. Do not be in a hurry to call an elder. Be sure of him first; keep the office pure. Take care of your own physical needs and work toward good health. You need to eat and have a healthy lifestyle to serve well.
2Tim 2:3-7	Be diligent; do your job well – achieve excellence.

	Soldier up – follow the chain of command; focus on the mission and keep others focused.
	Athlete up – train yourself and others (be serious about it).
	Farmer up – put your hand on the plow, trust God and don't look back.
2Tim 2:14	Lead with authority.
2 Tim 4:1-2	Keep people on track. Use the Word of God effectively to reprove, rebuke, and exhort with great patience and instruction.
Titus 2:15	Exercise authority as you teach, encourage, and rebuke.
Titus 1:2	Appoint elders to the office as may be needed to accomplish the work. Add to your number as the congregation and your need for help grows.
Heb 13:17	Keep watch over the souls of God's people. They are accountable to follow you, and you are accountable to God.
1Peter 5:1	Exercise oversight authority over the flock of God, always with their best interests in mind and never for personal gain.

Teaching (Preaching)

It means to proclaim the gospel and teach Scripture to the people. Teaching is far more than telling people what Scripture says: teaching also explains what it means and shows them how to apply it to their lives. Scripture is the basis for living a changed life in obedience to Christ. Far too many people are trying to change their lives by how they feel about things. Somehow they think they can know how to be a Christian on their own, apart from the Word of God and apart from being in relationship with mature believers. This is utter nonsense: "I think it's true, therefore it is."

The flock simply needs encouraged to become dedicated readers and students of the Word of God. It contains the blueprint for building a life of discipleship, and it is impossible to achieve a full life in Christ without it: *"Your word is a lamp unto my feet and a light for my path"* (Psalm 119:15). The pastor and teacher has donned the *"helmet of salvation"* and wields *"the sword of the Spirit, which is the Word of God"* (Ephesians 6:17).

Wield it well, for it is the basis of your authority as elder!

TABLE 3: TEACHING AND PREACHING DUTIES

SCRIPTURE	HOW THIS APPLIES TO PREACHING AND TEACHING
1Tim 2:9-15	Provide Biblical instruction to women in the church. Teach them to be an example of faith and love.
1Tim 4:1-6	Pay attention to what others are teaching your flock, recognize and correct errors, identify the source of the teaching and point it out to the people. Spend time in the Word of God to nourish yourself. Its teaching is sound. Use it to avoid confusion from false doctrines and myths.
1Tim 4:12	Be bold in proclaiming and teaching truth from the Word of God.
1Tim 4:13-14	Be faithful and consistent at reading, explaining, and applying the Word of God publicly.
1Tim 5:24-6:6	Do the hard work of teaching and preaching. This is how the people will learn to know the difference between truth and lies. Teach them how Christ wants them to live.
1Tim 6:7-11	Be free of the love of money. Teach people to put God and His kingdom first.
1Tim 6:13-16	Keep yourself true to the commands of Christ which we find in Scripture.
1Tim 6:17-19	Teach the wealthy not to be arrogant, to care for others, to do good works, and to be generous. Do not put hope in riches, but in God. Serve Him.
2Tim 1:8-11	Witness to others about salvation. Teach, testify, and preach. Never give up. Persevere through trials. Keep going.

2Tim 1:12-14 Endure suffering for the Gospel. Maintain the standard of teaching sound words. Guard the gift that has been given to you by the power of the Holy Spirit.

2Tim 2:2 Be a teacher of the truth as was passed on to you from the Apostles of old so that you may reproduce yourself as they reproduced themselves.

2Tim 2:8-13 Always remember who Christ is and what He did for us and pass this along through teaching to everyone. Even if you are put into prison for it, the Word of God will not be held in chains, so proclaim it.

2Tim 2:15-16 Handle Scripture accurately. Do not engage in useless conversation that leads to ungodliness. Stay focused.

2Tim 3:1-15 You will face difficulties. Face them with a deep knowledge of the Word of God. Teach it to others. His Word will show them the way. One needs to know it in order to teach it.

2Tim 3:16-17 Keep your flock on track. Scripture forms the basis for all legitimate ministries. Use it for teaching, correction, reproof, and training.

2Tim 4:1-2 Preach it, Pastor! Teach the Word of God in every season, during good times and bad. Use it for bringing correction, but be patient with all as you do so.

Titus 2:6 Similarly to the teaching of women, also teach young men to be self controlled.

Titus 2:7 Set an example both in your teaching and how you live it out. Have integrity.

James 3:1 Be careful how and what you teach. You will be judged more strictly than others. Do not presume to teach what you do not know.

Shepherding (Pastoring)

Shepherding means showing people how to live by setting an example for them to follow. The shepherd leads them down the right path, the path of discipleship that encourages people to grow into Christ-likeness. The shepherd balances oversight authority with "do as I do" rather than "do as I say." The shepherd protects, loves, encourages, and guides the flock. The shepherd leads them into worship and shows them how to do the work of ministry while also doing it alongside them. A shepherd encourages and mentors and guides the people on the path of Christ. A shepherd walks with the flock.

TABLE 4: SHEPHERDING AND PASTORING DUTIES

SCRIPTURE	HOW THIS APPLIES TO SHEPHERDING AND PASTORING
1Tim 2:1	Pray for the lost. Lead the members of your church into a life of habitual prayer for others.
1Tim 2:2-8	Lead the people to do the work of evangelism – guide them into discipleship.
1Tim 4:12	Be a model of virtue that makes it easy for people to follow you.
1Tim 4:15-16	Make regular consistent progress toward becoming like Christ. Others will follow you, so be sure to make progress.
1Tim 5:1-2	Be gracious and gentle as you confront sin that exists in the life of God's people. But do not ignore it: confront it.
1Tim 6:11-12	Pursue a life of godliness, faith, love, endurance and gentleness as you guide others toward doing the same. They should be following your example. Set a good one. Protect the flock. Fight for the faith against its enemies. Take hold of your faith. Be serious about it because others are watching you.
1Tim 6:13-16	Be obedient in your own behavior because you serve the Ruler of mankind.
1Tim 6:17-19	Encourage the wealthy to live for Christ. It is not about money, but about Him.

1Tim 6:20-21	Guard the truth. It has been entrusted to your care. Point people to a life that is truly a life worth living.
2Tim 1:6-7	Be enthusiastic and excited about the great gift of God. Enthusiasm is contagious: fan it into flames. Do not be timid about doing your job. The Spirit of God will work power through you.
2Tim 2:1	Remain of strong and upright character. You are leading by example.
2 Tim 2:22-26	Pursue righteous living, faith, and love. Do not get involved in philosophical or theological wrangling. Just proclaim the truth and lead others. Be teachable, coachable, kind, gentle, and patient even when you are wronged.
2Tim 4:5	Be sober in everything. Endure hardship (it will be hard). Do the work of an evangelist, for everyone should learn to evangelize. Lead people to Christ and show them how to lead others toward discipleship as you are doing (duplicate yourself).
James 5:12	Pray for the sick. Anoint them with oil. Visit people who are hurting. Encourage them.

If you are a senior pastor and feel that your primary strength is not in any of these three categories, and yet you are somehow in charge, don't worry! Instead, figure out how to supplement your shortcomings by finding qualified people to serve alongside you and under your leadership. Create a team that allows all the categories to be filled. It is up to you to do what you do best, while bringing other elders/pastors and leaders into a team who can work well together to accomplish the job. By serving well together, in a group where one's weakness is offset by another's strength, you can become, in effect, a whole pastor!

Having spent some time looking at the duties of elders, it should be clear why the Bible refers to them as having a noble task, a fine work.

> *"Here is a trustworthy saying: If anyone sets his heart on being an overseer, he desires a noble task* **(1 Timothy 3:1)**."

What a noble task it is. The importance of the job of elder cannot be overstated. A person should be compelled to do this work by God. We refer to it as "a calling." For those who are called to serve as an elder there will be a longing for the job, a desire of the heart that simply cannot be ignored. Be careful, though: don't seek the job without considering the costs. Hebrews 13:17 makes it abundantly clear that the elders will be held accountable for their accomplishments in leading the flock of God. Just as the flock is expected to obey, the elder is expected to lead well.

It is important to note that nobody has a full measure of experience and spiritual gifts in every area. This is why we need to learn to work together as a team. One elder will be especially good at teaching, but may fall short at shepherding or administration. One who is wonderful at being a shepherd may find the other categories difficult to fulfill. This is why the Bible spends more time on "character qualifications" than it does on "abilities or experience." I will spend time on the concept of teamwork in chapters 5 and 7. First, though, since the primary emphasis of Scripture for an elder's qualification is found in character, we should summarize the requirements.

A short list of character qualifications can be gleaned from a study of Paul's letters to Timothy and Titus.[79]

TABLE 5: SUMMARY OF CHARACTER QUALIFICATION OF THE ELDER

1Tim 3:2 and Titus 1:6-7

- **Above reproach or blameless**
    - There will be no hidden skeletons in the closet of the elder candidate. People will have no *legitimate* criticism of them. From the day of salvation forward there should be nothing that would disqualify them from service.
- **Married successfully**
    - The elder candidate should be in a committed monogamous marriage relationship with one spouse. The actual wording is "husband of one wife." The candidate should demonstrate loyalty, faithfulness, trust, and dedication in a successful relationship with one person.

1Tim 3:2

- **Temperate**
  - This implies strength in being focused on the job while exhibiting self control, especially in control of appetite for anything worldly.

1Tim 3:2 and Titus 1:8

- **Prudent.**
  - The elder is sensible, diligent, and careful, not rash.

1Tim 3:2

- **Respectable**
  - The elder is respected because of good behavior, having a sense of modesty, an ordered personality with decorum.

1Tim 3:2 and Titus 1:8

- **Hospitable**
  - The elder will extend hospitality to others. Often you will find the elder entertaining people at home because of a love of guests.

1Tim 3:2 and 2Tim 2:24

- **Must be able to teach**
  - A large part of the elder ministry is teaching people from the Word of God in order to apply Scripture, so they can "repent" and change how they live.

1Tim 3:3 and 2Tim 2:24

- **The Elder is gentle and loving.**
  - This is another way of saying they are "kind hearted." They will exhibit patience with people as they mentor them to do their work.
- **A lover of peace.**
- **Free of "the love of money."**
- **An elder has a deep love for Christ, His Word, and His people.**

1Tim 3:4

- **A good manager of his own household.**
  - How can an elder manage the family of God if unable to manage his own family well?

1Tim 3:6

- **Not a new convert.**
  - As discussed in this book, one should take time to prepare for ministry (sharpen your ax) before you begin. Maturity comes with effort. Don't be hasty to run out and become a pastor right after you say, "I believe!" There is much to learn first.

1Tim 3:7

- **A good reputation is enjoyed by the elder.**
  - People in the community who are not in the church should speak well of an elder.

2Tim 2:24

- **Not resentful.**
  - The Elder will not resent the blessing or gifts received by others, but will rejoice with them. Even after being persecuted or wronged, the elder will not carry resentment in the heart. In other words, patience is exhibited when wronged.

Titus 1:6

- **A believing family**
  - Elders will have been successful at proclaiming the Good News at home. Their children will also believe in Christ for their salvation.

Titus 1:7

- **A servant's heart**
  - The elder is a servant who is concerned with the needs of others, and is not self willed. A person who focuses on his own needs, satisfaction, goals, and the pursuit of a career is not a servant of others.

- **Not quick to anger**
  - Temper is kept in check and remains under control

Titus 1:8

- **A lover of good things**
  - Good is a relative term. Here it refers to the things of God. An elder loves good things and is devout or devoted to these good things of God. The elder maintains self control and is just and fair in dealing with others.

One identified as having these character traits is qualified to be an elder. If called to serve, nothing should keep them from serving. In fact, the elder should be honored and well provided for by the people being shepherded. The key is to take care in identifying these traits before selecting anyone to serve as an elder. I strongly recommend the appointment be considered carefully. Existing elders should be in charge and in control of the process. Anyone exhibiting these character traits and doing their very best to function as a shepherd leader would be a joy for people to follow.[80] At least one would certainly think so.

When you consider the list of duties the elder has (described above), there should be a check in your heart that begs the question, "How on earth can I ever accomplish all these things?" The answer is, "You are not able, but Christ is." I am convinced that the work will be done through you by the Holy Spirit. This Spirit intends for elders to exercise their unique one of a kind set of spiritual gifts in relationship with others: those having different gifts and abilities, working in cooperation with each other.

It is in this fashion that the "Body of Christ" is formed, and it is in our relationship with each other that the mission will be accomplished (1 Corinthians 12). Scripture typically refers to elders in the plural for good reason. In my opinion, it is by working together they become, in effect, "a whole pastor" and a model to the congregation. Elders should be committed to working together as an effective ministry team and applying the Word of God. As they live it out together, watch the power of His Spirit go to work in your church: for "None of us is as smart as all of us!"[81]

Summary of Elders' Responsibility and Role

The Most Important Role: Teaching Sound Doctrine and Mentoring Others

The most significant and important role an elder must fulfill is that of "teacher of sound doctrine while mentoring others toward maturity." Disciples don't just happen; they are taught Scripture and shown how to live for Christ. The authority vested to the office of elder is found primarily in the requirement of teaching. One cannot overstate the importance of teaching and mentoring as elders accomplish their purpose.

> When the minister of the gospel faces the Lord God as judge, there will be many questions addressed to him, many standards of accountability, and many criteria of judgment. In the end, however, the most essential criterion of judgment for the minister of God will be, "Did you preach the word? Did you fully carry out the ministry of the Word? In season and out of season, was the priority of your ministry the preaching of the Word?"
>
> Of course this is not to say that there are not other issues, other responsibilities, and even other priorities. But it is to say that there is only one central, nonnegotiable, immovable, and essential priority, and that is the preaching of the Word of God.[82]
>
> "Far too many pastors assume that the authority they enjoy is their own, that they somehow earned it or achieved it."
>
> In the end the central purpose of every Christian ministry is to make known the Word of God. This is accomplished by the proclaiming, teaching and preaching of it and is above everything else. [83]

As such, because teaching is the specific assigned purpose of the elder, the elders' oversight authority is derived from it. Everything that goes on in the church should be to serve and support the proclaiming of the truth contained in God's Word. This ministry is above all and goes well beyond telling people what do to. It requires showing them how to live a full life in Christ. A member's part in this is to become a dedicated student of the Word, learning from those selected to be their elders. Application of Scripture is for the purpose of changing one's approach to living, which is another way of saying, "repent."

A Bus Driver or a Ship's Captain?

I have heard two analogies regarding the role of an elder. One is that of a bus driver. The other is of a captain of a ship. I prefer the ship analogy.

A bus driver lets the people on board, has a predetermined destination, and a route to take. The driver is well trained for the job and knows exactly where to go and how to get there. The passengers are expected to sit comfortably in their seats and enjoy the ride. They will go wherever the bus driver takes them. If they do not want to go, they are free to get off the bus. Clearly, the driver is in charge and the people are expected to follow. I do not care much for this description.

Consider instead a beautiful and fully rigged sailing ship as an analogy for a local congregation. A ship like this is safe while anchored in the harbor, but that is not what ships are for. The owner is Christ, and He most certainly desires to see the ship out on the open sea at full sail, taking risks, relying upon Him even when the weather is rough and the waves are frightful. The world is full of people who are lost at sea. They are living without regard for God and unaware of the salvation available through Christ. The sailors on board the ship are responsible for search and rescue operations as lost souls are encountered along the way, as they go about their daily lives. It is a dangerous work, to be sure. The crew can expect to endure long hours and hardship. The work takes them outside their comfort zone, but is highly rewarding.

At the helm of the ship is the one who has been given the responsibility of overseeing and steering, teaching and equipping, shepherding and guiding. In addition, many other responsibilities need to be attended to in order for the ship to function properly and run smoothly. The crew needs to be taught how to do their jobs and provided with the resources they need to accomplish them. Sails need mending, supplies managed, lines spliced, food prepared, the deck cleaned, money and resources allocated, equipment maintained, rescued souls ministered to, and the sick healed. The ship should have a sense of order, a chain of command, and a spirit of teamwork and cooperation if it is to function well and survive the journey while accomplishing its mission. A hymn of praise, like the sea shanties of old, shall be on their lips as they work by each others' side.

As the work of rescue is accomplished, new people will be added to the ranks of the crew; they need trained. Everyone is expected to do a job, for which they need to be equipped. Some will help and serve. Some will teach and train. Some will fill positions of leadership, being placed by rank over a ministry. Some will become captains themselves. The work is hard and treacherous, and though no one will survive the journey, everyone who joins the crew will live on to tell the tale in their true home, which is not here.

Until then, their camaraderie and team work will be illustrated by the love the captain and crew have for one another. Scripture uses the term "elder" to describe the person whose job it is to man the helm of this good ship. The elders should man it well and the people should follow them, serving wholeheartedly as they work together to achieve the great commandment and commission:

Love God with all you have – Love others as yourself

Evangelism – Identification – Discipleship

Are you going yet? Is it time to "pull up the anchor and set sail?" Do you have yourself organized properly? Are you managed well? There is no "I" in "Team."

CHAPTER 5

We have different gifts, according to the grace given us. If a man's gift is prophesying, let him use it in proportion to his faith. If it is serving, let him serve; if it is teaching, let him teach; if it is encouraging, let him encourage; if it is contributing to the needs of others, let him give generously; if it is leadership, let him govern diligently; if it is showing mercy, let him do it cheerfully.

Romans 12:6-8

Organization and Structure

In the case of any congregation, it would seem only natural for some degree of leadership and organization to exist. The Bible supports organization. Surely, modern human resources management would support the concept of, at a minimum, one member of the group functioning as the team leader, along with delegation of tasks according to each member's spiritual gifts and some hierarchy within the group.

Achieving Balance in the Three General Categories of Elder Responsibility

Administration - Teaching - Shepherding

As we have seen, an elder has three primary categories of responsibility. Each area requires some degree of giftedness to be good at it. We generally refer to them as the spiritual gifts of administration, teaching, and shepherding. Some people might also include other gifts, including mercy. These gifts will never exist in equal measure within any one person. Each person is unique. Elders gifted most in "administration" should spend the majority of their time involved in managing the big picture and keeping people on track. Delegate the job of "shepherding the flock" to those who are most gifted in shepherding, care and mercy, allowing them to spend the majority of their time within that role. Allow those most gifted in the area of "teaching and preaching" to spend the majority of their time doing so. Through good teamwork, all three areas can be done well.

Personally, I like the use of various terms to describe the division of labor. Meetings need to be run; people and resources need to be organized. Disciples need to be deployed for doing the work of ministry. This is best accomplished by putting administrative elders/pastors in place for the job, working in cooperation with a dedicated group of servants from the church to whom tasks can be delegated. Servants may include paid staff, along with members of a board of some kind along with a variety of ministry leaders.

As we have seen, the teaching and preaching ministry is extremely important to the success of the mission. This ministry is best accomplished by placing gifted teaching elders/pastors in the job. Certainly some folks in the church will be gifted teachers, but will not be called to be elders. Put them to work in the teaching ministry, too, but under the elders' authority and direction. Elders need to be diligent to see that sound doctrine is being taught at all levels, from the pulpit, to small groups, in children's ministry, and in adult Bible study. At the same time, we must present the Bible in ways that will reach people where they are without doing so in a way that becomes a barrier to their hearing and understanding of God's Word. If your church has a small group ministry (I hope it does), it needs to be kept on track, so that it is leading people into full life with Christ, "making them into disciples."

Finally, many other important tasks need to be done, including hospital visitation, counseling, caring, encouragement, prayer, and worship, to name just a few. The flock needs not only to be told what to do, but also shown how to do it by those who are willing to do it with them. This ministry is best accomplished by putting shepherding elders/pastors in place, working alongside the people themselves, who are encouraged to serve the needs of others. In time, mature disciples will be sent out on their own to show others how to be disciples. Of the three categories, it is my opinion that a church is in need of more shepherds than any other group. The number of shepherding elders and ministers should grow in proportion to the number of people who need to be shepherded. One possible way to achieve this is by having mature members who have the gifts of shepherding and mercy assigned to work with the shepherding elder team. Perhaps these folks should be your mentors, small group leaders and care ministry members.

In time, it is possible that the some of the folks assigned to work alongside the various elders will become elders/pastors too. All elders/pastors should be expected to perform the duties of each of these ministries to one degree or another. It's just that each one will be far more effective when they are positioned to spend the *majority* of their time in areas of their highest gifts. To be effective, caring teamwork is not only vital but far more productive.

> *"Two are better than one, because they have a good return for their work: If one falls down, his friend can help him up. But pity the man who falls and has no one to help him up!" (**Ecclesiastes 4:9-10**).*

Two people working well together should be able to accomplish more than twice as much as they could accomplish separately. Imagine how effective an entire congregation can be when organized well, in a culture that expects caring relationships. Effective teamwork brings better results because it allows each member to focus on what they are most gifted to do. Did I mention joy? If you are currently an elder or pastor or ministry leader, ask yourself a question: "How would I describe what I currently experience the most in my work: joy or grief?" If "joy" is not the first word to come to your mind, perhaps you are a square peg being forced into a round hole. Address it. Or, it may be that shepherding your congregation is like trying to herd cats. Get help. Teach them. You may be the chief cat herder!

Proper organization allows elders the freedom to spend most of their time doing the things that God has uniquely equipped them to do. Much joy will come from doing the jobs they are most gifted for because it is both what they love and what they do best. For this to happen, the church must have a good organizational structure, good management, and division of labor. It could be represented in a variety of different organizational charts, though I will attempt to provide examples for you. Whatever works for your church is fine, provided you remain true to Scripture. The Word of God provides clear evidence of flexibility for change and adaptation within the structure it has provided. The goal of the organization should be to achieve balance in all three categories of responsibility. They all need to be done well to achieve the mission.

Find an effective combination of the talents and spiritual gifts of those who serve together as elders/pastors, as well as members who work with them. Every elder will have some giftedness in each category, but will have scored higher in one and lower in another. For example, my personal spiritual gifts, in order from highest to lowest are teaching, followed by leadership and administration, then shepherding and exhortation. I am a more effective pastor when I can be teamed up with others who score high in the gift of mercy and helps. Together, we make a whole pastor: by myself, it is much more of a struggle.

Ideally, you should strive to build an elder/pastor team, with mature believers working alongside them, in order to achieve an optimal blend of these important spiritual gifts. The following table illustrates one possible model for an effective team:

TABLE 6: Balancing Spiritual Gifts to be a "Whole Pastor"

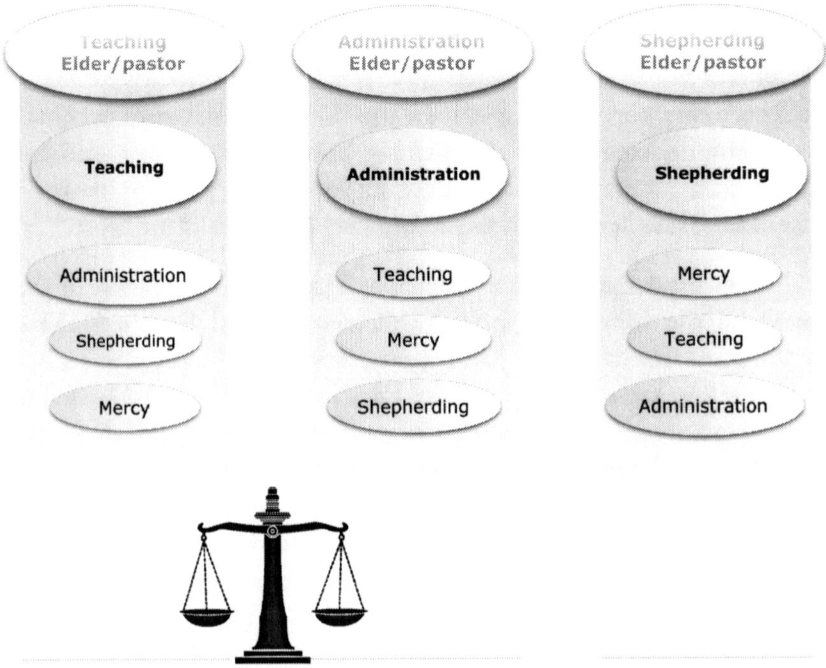

This chart is not intended to be an exhaustive list of gifts that should be held by an elder/pastor or other ministry leader. One might correctly ask, "What about the gifts of evangelism or helps or others, too?" You may have a pastor whose primary strength is "evangelism," but has none of the other gifts listed on the chart above. That is the point! It is in an effective organization of people who have different gifts that allow them to accomplish the job of shepherding as they work well together as a team.

Today, in an attempt to figure out how to succeed in ministry, many churches are taking time to collect all kinds of data and questionnaires from their members. Some make the mistake of asking members, most of whom are new believers, to answer questions they do not have the answers to. Be careful to be clear about your mission and purpose, not seeking direction, but rather giving it. You should lead them and not the other way around. Questionnaires may even include spiritual gifts analysis. If so, what follows? What is implemented or changed after the data is collected? I submit that doing an analysis or completing a questionnaire just for the sake of accumulating data, or to try and figure out what to do, is a useless exercise. It should have a purpose designed to help accomplish the mission, and it is our job as elders/pastors to know what that mission is. These things should make a difference and help you become more effective. After the analysis is done, we need to be sure to follow up and place people into jobs and ministries they are most suited for.

Often new members will be put through a series of classes or a process of membership that can take weeks to complete. Truly there should be some path that purposely connects people steadily toward a life lived well for Christ, a life built on relationship with others that leads toward maturity, discipleship, and even leadership. This is great, and it is part of being a disciple. At some point in the process, new members may do a spiritual gifts inventory designed to help them know what they are suited for. This final step may be accompanied by great fanfare and presentations by various ministries. However, if the ball is dropped at the administrative level and these good folks are not followed up with, invited to participate, and plugged into a ministry in which to serve, they will eventually fall off the radar and may even disappear. Some folks will be aggressive and will go after ministry involvement or join a small group. Most folks will wait to be asked. For that reason, the administrative team needs to know who they are, understand what ministry of service they are best suited for, and find a way to invite them to participate, helping them make connections. Otherwise, why go through the process? Is it just to have the data stored in a computer?

Pastor Rick Warren calls this a process of understanding your **SHAPE** (a combination of **S**piritual Gifts, **H**eart, **A**bilities, **P**ersonality, and **E**xperience).[84] The idea is to find a way for people to serve God by plugging them into a ministry for which they are uniquely "Shaped." Do we model this at the top? Not always, but we should. Elders/pastors would do well to consider how to arrange themselves in a manner that improves their effectiveness together, while helping members do the same. If giftedness is allowed to shape the teamwork at the top, it will infiltrate the rest of the body as everyone chips in to serve. But the process will be more successful when it is well managed. It must become part of your culture.

The goal here is to learn how to work together in a way that maximizes each person's spiritual gifts. In a small church, the pastor would do well to identify mature members of the congregation who have the character qualifications to serve as elder, a willingness to learn, and spiritual gifts in areas where the pastor is lacking them. Put qualified people on your elder board, let others serve as deacons or as ministry leaders, and have them work alongside you. Try to achieve a balance that will allow all the work of the elder to be accomplished with excellence. In a large church, you probably have multiple pastors and/or elders. Be sure to organize them effectively and help each other do the job. I encourage your elders to be engaged in the work of shepherding your people while walking with them, helping them through their dark times and equipping them to serve others.

In either case (large or small church), delegate specific jobs to each elder/pastor of your church to allow each one to do the job each is most gifted to do. Everyone's time is limited. You will get better results when your limited amount of time is spent doing the things God gifted you for. Pray for guidance. I believe Scripture calls us to function in this manner, and that the Holy Spirit will answer your prayers for effective teamwork and balance. For a representation of this balance, see the table below.

TABLE 7: Balanced Elder/Pastor Team

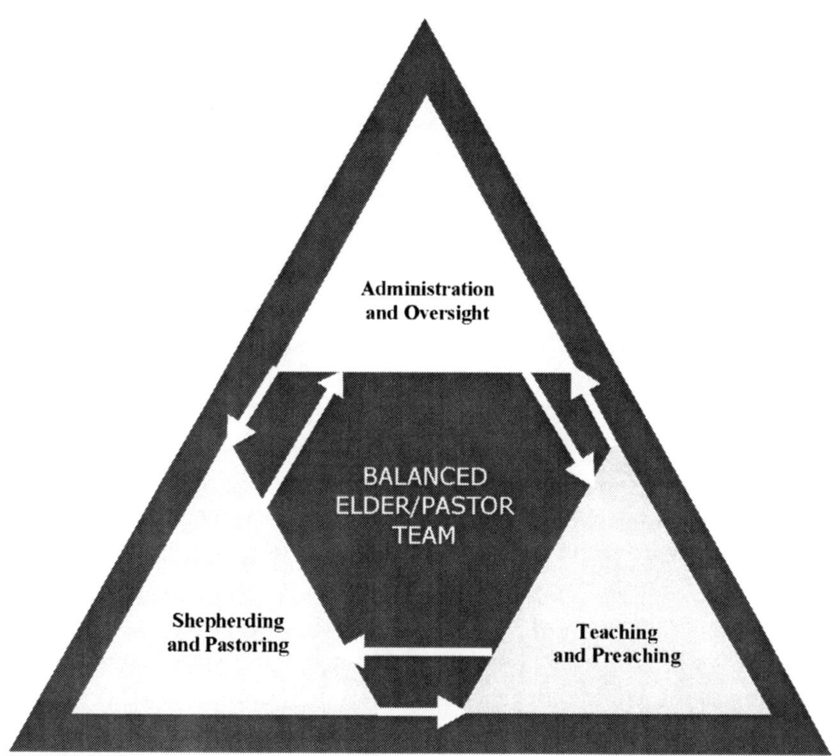

What would it look like in terms of an organizational chart? I would like to provide a picture to help you visualize the lines of authority. This picture is an attempt to capture the essence of the Scripture's teaching on church government. It is difficult because there is no one size fits all. No congregation is the same as any other, and each one has its own community and culture in which to minister. Every church has its own unique mix of people, spiritual gifts, shortcomings, needs, opportunities, and resources. The Bible provides flexibility here: each congregation should respond and adapt to its own community and ministry needs based on what it has available to work with. In general, though, organization can be pictured.

The next three tables show possible ways to illustrate an organizational chart for small and large churches. These are not intended to be the only way to illustrate it. You can feel free to use these as a starting point for designing your own. Just be sure to identify the Biblical chain of command and authority within your structure. In addition, be clear about the meaning of the words you use to refer to people who are leaders in your church. Stay as true to the Bible as you are able.

Terms can be confusing when used haphazardly. In this book I attempt to provide clear definitions for many of them. For example, elder, pastor, deacon, bishop, minister, and overseer have clear Biblical definitions. Today, the evangelical church is using a whole variety of additional terms. More often than not, they mean different things to different people. Often, their meaning is found more in a modern understanding than in a Scriptural one. I know of one Gen X church that does not use the term "pastor" at all. Instead, their head elders are given the title "Coriolis." Huh? Apparently, "coriolis" has something to do with the effect of uneven heating of the earth. How does this apply Scripture to our understanding?

One should always start with what a word meant at the time the Scripture was written and apply the original meaning to our understanding, rather than the other way around. Doing so allows us to govern and organize ourselves in a way that is more closely aligned with the Word of God. I ask you: how can we possibly go wrong by trying our best to operate according to the original instructions found in Scripture? Doesn't it make sense that it would be better to bring Scripture forward into our culture to change our thinking, rather than taking our culture and thinking backwards and applying it to Scripture?

TABLE 8: Sample Organizational Chart (Small Church)

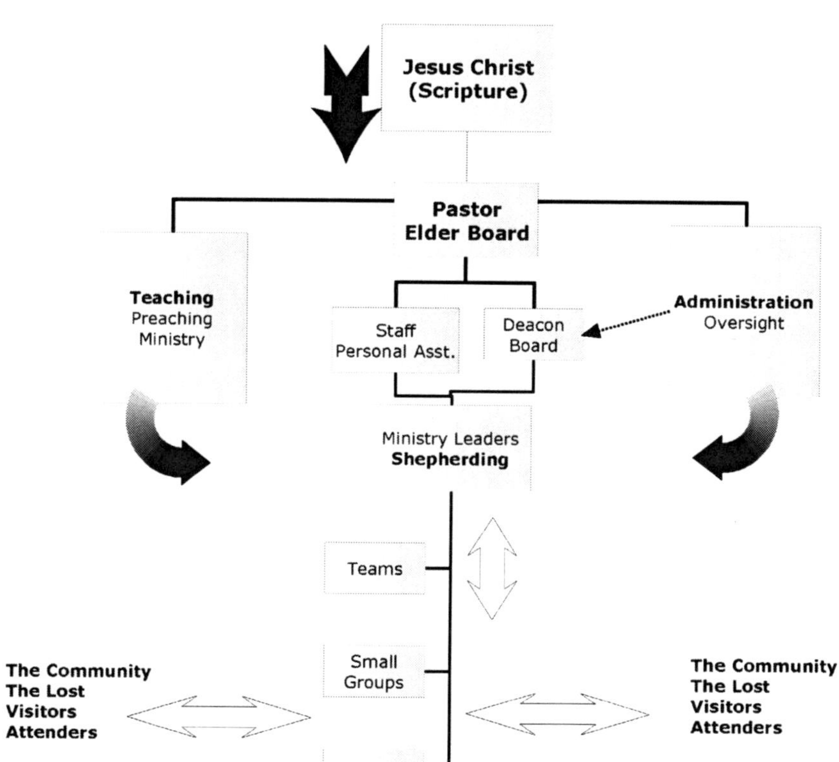

The small church has a problem. The pastor is expected to do nearly everything. You run the risk of burning your pastor out with unrealistic expectations. The church needs to find a way to free their elder (pastor) for the ministry of the Word. He needs (and wants) to teach you how to live for Christ as His disciples and needs your help. Members and/or deacons need to serve their elder/pastor and each other, taking details away from his responsibility so the elder/pastor can focus on delegating tasks while teaching and leading you into maturity. Each member is responsible to live as a "disciple," evangelizing, ministering to those who are sick and in need, serving, and loving one another. The care and shepherding ministry will burn out a pastor more quickly than any other. There are too many people in great need for one person to handle. Your shepherding or care pastor needs a great team of care ministers to achieve this job. Help each other, and do what your pastor asks you to do. It will help greatly and bring a joy that will spill into your lives. The elder's (pastor's) job is to equip you to do these works of service, so do them. It is not your pastor's job to do the work for you.

TABLE 9: Sample Organizational Chart (Larger Church)

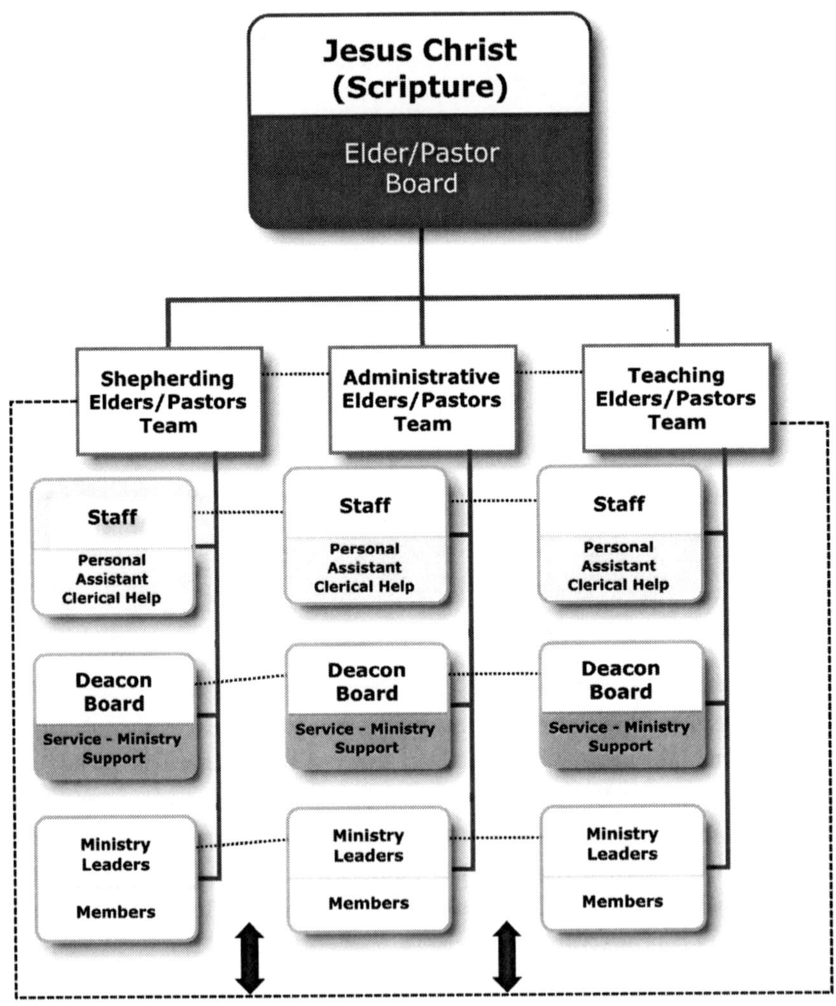

The danger in a large church is that people can get lost in the shuffle. It is amazing to me to see so many folks attending church regularly but literally hiding out in the crowd without becoming involved in deep, Christ centered relationships. When this happens, the church fails to shepherd them along the path of discipleship. The organization needs to have a system that allows people to be in relationship with each other while moving toward maturity in their faith. Administration and teaching can be accomplished by smaller teams of elders, but shepherding cannot. Because of the importance of relationships, a single elder can only shepherd a limited number of people effectively. It becomes important to figure out how to duplicate more shepherds who become engaged with the flock, under supervision and guidance from the shepherding elders/pastors. Here, the shepherding pastors need to work hard at building relationships with smaller groups of people and training them to shepherd other groups of people. The small group model may be an appropriate way to organize this important ministry. Helping people from the large crowd make a connection to a small group can be challenging. Many people like hiding. Some folks will need an opportunity to participate in a smaller crowd as an interim step before getting connected with a good small group. Consider offering some form of teaching and training program that allows people to participate in groups of 50 before committing to a group of 10. It's all about making connections that gradually increase one's comfort with the kind of intimacy Christ wants His people to have with each other. Ultimately, your future leaders should be drawn from those who have grown and matured in the small group ministry setting.

How many people can one elder effectively shepherd? It depends on how much time they have, but let's imagine the number is twenty people, though it may be more. If these people are trained to be shepherd leaders and they in turn can be put in charge of a small group of ten people each, then you have just multiplied the shepherding elder's impact from twenty people to two hundred people. So, in a church of one thousand members, using my example, you would need to have five shepherding elders in place. Each of them needs to manage twenty shepherd leaders, who each manage ten people. Training and mentoring come from the top down as people grow in maturity and discipleship. Just how many shepherds you need depends on how many people are in your church, how fast you are growing, and how many members one elder can really mentor well. In fact, this team or small group ministry may form a wonderful training ground to raise new shepherding elders from among your members.

More on this, including diagrams to help you catch a vision for multiplying ministry, will be found in Chapter 7 of this book.

TABLE 10 Sample Organizational Chart (Other)

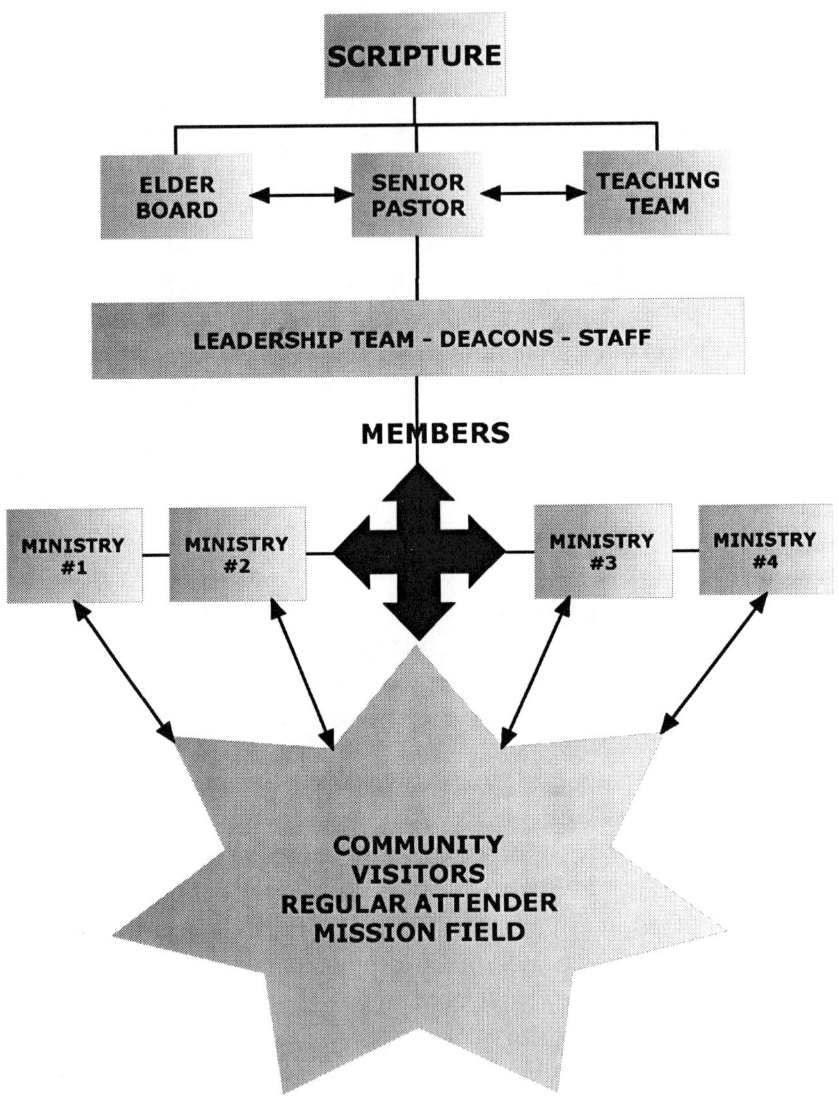

Here in Table 10 I am trying here to represent an organization with checks and balances between the elder board and the pastors, coordinated by a senior pastor or lead elder. Oversight, administration and teaching authority under Scripture is a team effort. A leadership team consisting of mature leaders, deacons, and administrative personnel are managed for the purpose of achieving the vision and mission of the church through various approved ministries. Members are encouraged to grow and mature while being put to work in a ministry that helps identify their unique SHAPE and calling while putting them to work in their best fit ministry.

The chart shows only four ministries, but there could be many more. Ministries could include the following: children's programs, Bible study, leadership development, evangelism, resource management, church life, fellowship groups, finance and giving, worship, creative arts, missions, and community outreach.

Putting the Structure into Action.

Now that we have seen a few ideas on structure for organizing church government, we should consider what it looks like as a church goes into action. Scripture paints a wonderful picture of elders and members of the flock working together in loving relationships. Each person should be encouraged to serve in a ministry where they can exercise their own unique spiritual gifts and temperament, which contributes to achieving the mission. Elders work to teach and guide them in the way of discipleship. Deacons serve both the people and their elders. Everyone is going and making disciples as all grow in maturity, and some become leaders themselves. Remember, it should resemble the crew of a ship more than the passengers on a bus.

This whole process is pictured in the Book of Acts. The church was new, and Peter had been preaching the message about repentance and baptism. The church grew as many people were being added to their number. The people dedicated themselves to learning and working together with their elders to achieve the mission. Read what it says,

> *"They devoted themselves to the apostles' teaching and to the fellowship, to the breaking of bread and to prayer. Everyone was filled with awe, and many wonders and miraculous signs were done by the apostles. All the believers were together and had everything in common. Selling their possessions and goods, they gave to anyone as he had need. Every day they continued to meet together in the temple courts. They broke bread in their homes and ate together with glad and sincere hearts, praising God and enjoying the favor of all the people. And the Lord added to their number daily those who were being saved"* (Acts 2:42-47).

Acts chapter 6 makes evident why this growth resulted in the need for deacons. I will address the subject of deacons shortly.

We have seen that Peter referred to himself as "a fellow Elder" (1 Peter 5:1) and that the apostles placed elders in charge of every church. What caught my eye in Acts chapter 2 was the dedication they had to each other. This is hardly a picture of some Grand Poopah in charge and "lording it over" the people. Nor is it a picture of a congregation making all the decisions or sitting on their laurels and watching others do the work. No, this is a picture of mature people, serious disciples, working together in a spirit of cooperation, sharing what they have, following, obeying and putting into action what they have learned through the application of God's Word as taught by their elders. You can observe five things being done well by this New Testament church: fellowship, discipleship, worship, ministry, and evangelism! All the components of the five purposes given by Christ are being accomplished as they function well as a body of believers. They followed God's organizational structure, and the result was growth: growth in maturity **and** growth in numbers. We should strive to do the same and our emphasis should be on maturity and discipleship while growth will take care of itself.

Growth is certainly the desire and expectation of God. Growth is the reality of what the New Testament church actually achieved. In this passage we should note that it was God who added to their number as each person contributed to the effort of the team. When we do our part, living as He instructed, the result will be for God to add to our number. New people need to be trained. Pastor Rick Warren provides a good summary of the kind of growth expected in what he calls "The Five Dimensions of Church Growth."[85]

Churches grow:

1. Warmer through fellowship.
2. Deeper through discipleship.
3. Stronger through worship.
4. Broader through ministry.
5. Larger through evangelism.

The result described in Acts confirms that the early church was accomplishing the mission: *"They dedicated themselves to the teaching"* **and**

"The Lord added to their number daily." Many large churches today have failed to create a culture that expects changed lives, growth in maturity and commitment to the Word of God.

The following table attempts to illustrate what an Acts 2 church may look like, within the organizational structure provided by Scripture.

TABLE 11: Working Together (Elders, Deacons, Members)

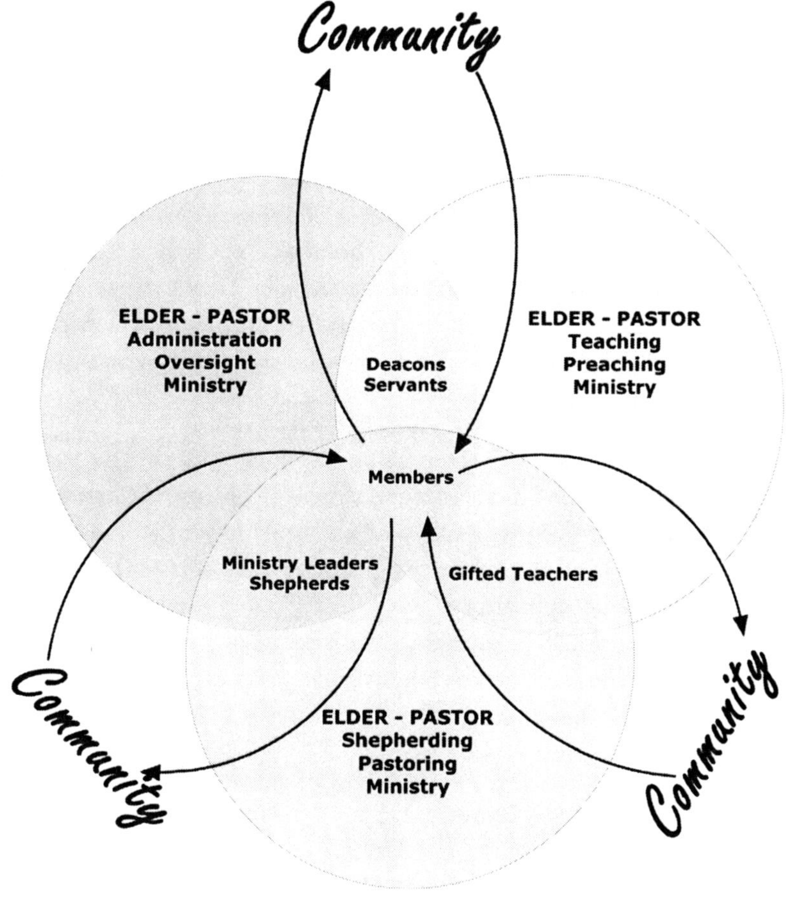

The Disciple Making Pastor.

Want to start an argument? Ask pastors and church leaders to answer the following questions: What is the role of the senior or

> lead pastor? Are various Biblical models equally valid? Is there a prescribed pastoral job description that emerges as a top priority? Want to escalate a proper theological debate into a shouting match? Then propose that the pastor is a specialist, primarily a teacher/equipper. Assert that he is called to work with the strong more than the weak, and that by training the well, he takes better care of and strengthens the weak. It is, in fact, true that the only real hope for the weak is the disciple-making pastor's multiplying his influence through the preparation of Christians for the work of service.[86]

Hopefully, I have successfully demonstrated who an elder is and what an elder does. The elder/pastor is responsible for preparing Christians for service. The elder needs to train those who are capable of serving, becoming the hands and feet of Jesus so that people who are lost and in need will be shown the love of Christ. I have shown that the Bible often refers to elders in the plural form because there is no set number of them; we need as many as are needed for the job. They have the primary responsibilities of teaching, administration, and shepherding. These three categories form the means by which they fulfill their job in accomplishing the mission statement.

We have considered both the mission statement and the five purposes of the church. From the Great Commandment (Matthew 22), we identify the first two as "love God with all you have" and "love others as yourself" (God first, me last). After the first two purposes, "Love God, love people," we find the three components of the Great Commission (Matthew 28), defined as evangelism, identification, and discipleship.[87] It is the expectation in Scripture that the flock will be taught how to accomplish the purpose of the church as they mature under the direction of their elders, while doing life together.

We have defined some important terms and considered how the church should be governed and organized. We have a mission to accomplish. Our desire to accomplish it will flow out of our love for God and others. In fact, unless God is our first love and our first priority, and without love for His people above ourselves, we cannot achieve the mission He gave us. Evangelism is defined as "going and making disciples." A disciple is defined as "one who has identified with Christ and is committed to the application of Scripture in order to learn how to follow and obey Him."

Pastor Bill Hull gave an excellent description of a process by which the church may achieve its purpose.[88] I have summarized it in the following chart and applied it to the three elder categories I have presented in this book.

The process has three steps:

1. Tell them what: Tell them why (Teaching)
2. Show them how: Do it with them (Shepherding)
3. Let them do it: Deploy them (Administration)

TABLE 12: The disciple making process

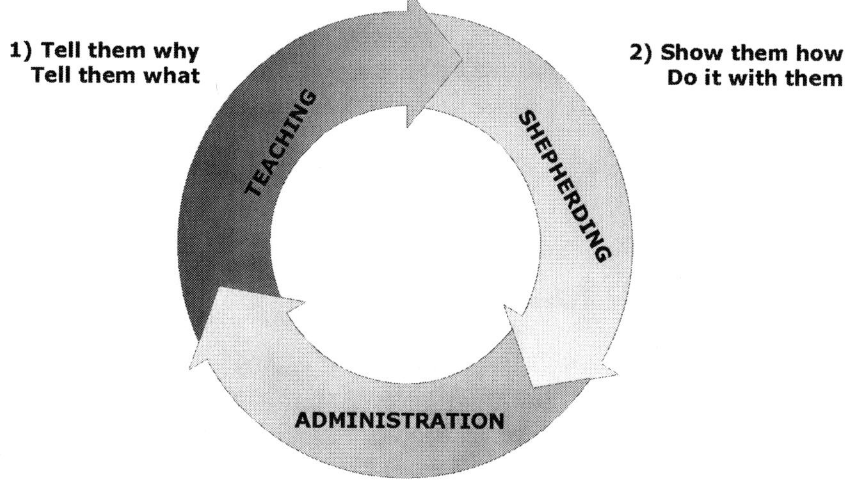

If we are to accomplish the purpose to *"Go therefore and make disciples…,"* we need to improve our understanding of the process. It really is a big job and takes a life of dedication. Evangelism is not the job of only elders: it is everybody's job. The elder teaches and equips people to do it. This process is why the elder has authority in God's system of church government, and everyone has the duty to serve.

As we will see in the next chapter, acts of "service" became so important in the New Testament church that a new office was created just to accommodate it: the office of "deacon," a ministry of serving.

CHAPTER 6

Hey, what is the stuff called that provides lubrication to help an engine run smoothly, keep from overheating, work well and last for a long time?

In the engine of the church, it is called "The deacon!"

- Jim Kirkland

For those who serve well as deacons gain a good standing for themselves and also great confidence in the faith that is in Christ Jesus

(ESV 1 Timothy 3:13)[89]

Defining the Word "Deacon"

Deacons are mature "disciples," who are trained in Scripture, able to articulate their faith, dedicated to serving others, and have become qualified to serve in an office. This office serves to help both elders and members accomplish tasks and ministry. Deacons are the lubrication that makes the church run smoothly! These are the folks that make sure the "things" associated with managing church grounds, finances, and many other items are done well. One could use the term broadly to describe any mature disciple of Christ who serves within the church in any capacity, for all are called to serve. In that sense, everyone is a deacon. When used in connection with a church office, though, the term applies especially to those who are members of a specific ministry team, working alongside the elders and subject to their oversight authority.

According to Scripture, a person selected for the special office or job of serving is to be a mature disciple having specific character qualifications (1 Timothy 3:8-13). They should be full of faith and the Holy Spirit (Acts

6:5), have knowledge of Scripture, and be able to communicate it as part of sharing their faith. To see this truth in action, one need go no further than to the story of one of the first servants appointed to the job of freeing the elders for their work, that of Stephen, who also became the first martyr. I encourage you to read his story, but especially his testimony that resulted in his death by stoning (Acts, chapter 7). Oh, that we would be so capable of sharing our faith from knowing the Word of God as well as Stephen! And he serves as a model to show us what a true deacon is, regardless of the term your church may use to describe the office.

The Appendix provides a detailed study of διάκονος (pronounced diakonos), the word from which we get "deacon." When it appears in its noun form it means simply one who is a servant or minister. In its verb form, it refers to the act of serving or ministering. Throughout the Bible we find the word used as "serving" and as "servant." The word is used in the New Testament nearly one hundred times. When considered in context, Scripture implies several possible meanings listed as follows (The Appendix provides a specific Scripture references for each example):

SERVING (Verb)

- Serving: As in *ministering* or caring for the needs of people.
- Serving: As in sending financial support in *relief* of brothers or a ministry.
- Serving: As in the elders' commitment to work hard at the *ministry* of teaching the Word of God.
- Serving: As in the service rendered by ministering angels who are sent by God to *help* those who are being saved.
- Serving: As a picture of the *kind of leadership* expected of elders who have been given oversight authority over the household of God.

SERVANT (Noun)

- Servant: As in a *servant* who carries out the wishes of one who has authority over them, like a slave under a master; a subject under a king, an employee under an employer, or as disciples under Christ.

- Servant: As in a good or faithful *minister.*
- Servant: As in a person who is working toward the achievement of a specific objective or mission which may be called a *"ministry"* or *"ministry of service"* and may include some amount of management responsibility.
- Servant: As in a person who *waits upon tables*; a waiter or waitress who serves food and drink.
- Servant: As in a *government official* with authority to punish and reward.
- Servant: As in a *deacon* who occupies a church office by the same name.

Defining "Deacon," with Help from Theological Dictionaries and Lexicons[90]

Evidence from historical records suggests the term was used in connection with an office, even in ancient times. In 100 B.C. a religious document lists various temple officials, including the "deacon" who served under and at the direction of the priests. Other ancient documents link the deacon to the office of priest, accountable to the priests but having management authority for the work delegated to them.[91]

In general, when we speak of serving, we are implying work being done on behalf of someone else, either voluntarily or under compulsion. The activity of serving is not the same thing as ruling. In fact, there is a sharp contrast between them. Scripture refers to serving in a humble manner, as opposed to one who serves in a prideful way.

According to *The Dictionary of New Testament Theology,* sometimes the New Testament replaces the word "deacon" with υπηρεται (pronounced huperete), which originally meant an assistant or under rower on a ship. From this word it may be possible to deduce the meaning of a servant helper or attendant who serves to assist someone in authority. In any case, there can be no doubt that a "servant" works to help someone else. The work of deacon eventually became an official office within the New Testament church. However, Scripture does not clearly state what the duties of the deacon are. We can correctly assume the deacons' work involves the act of serving, though in an official capacity. In a more specialized sense, in the New Testament church a deacon becomes involved with the material care of the church body while working closely with the office of overseer (elder) and serving under their direction. In the Ancient Orthodox Church, deacon became a paid position. In the Roman Catholic Church, deacon became a transitional step on the way to becoming a priest. [92]

It is compelling to observe the Greek grammar used by Paul when he singles out the people who served in the office of deacon, saying:

> *"Paul and Timothy, servants of Christ Jesus, To all the saints in Christ Jesus at Philippi, together with the overseers and deacons"* (Philippians 1:1).

The order of his greeting was "the saints," followed by "the overseers and deacons." Here Paul links the two coordinated offices of elder, called "overseer" in this passage, and deacon together. The grammar is similar to *"the pastors and teachers"* found in Ephesians 4 as I discussed in chapter 3 of this book. Here the language suggests two offices working in cooperation, linked together for a purpose.

The qualifications for serving in the office of deacon are quite similar to the qualifications for an elder. Like elders, deacons should be blameless and upright, not liars or given to loose living. They should manage their household well and be married to only one spouse. Their primary job is to serve in administration and practical service. It is my belief that the management of "tasks" associated with serving fall to the office of deacon. However, deacons do not only manage tasks, since they will often need to know how to manage people on their team. Also, it does not mean that an elder should have no tasks to manage, only people. In general, I believe an elder/pastor should mostly manage people, while a deacon helps the elder by mostly managing the "things" that need done for the church to function well.

The creation of the office itself may be described in Acts chapter 6:1-6, though we cannot be certain of it. All of the earliest sources of information on the deacon link the office with the elder or overseer, and they were never separated from each other. The deacon is both the servant of the church and the servant of the overseer. Evidence may exist to show that deacons worked with and for elders even in the early Jewish synagogue. The Christian offices of both elder and deacon, with the deacons serving at the direction of the elders and in support of them, seem a natural progression as the church grew.[93] The deacon is first and foremost "a servant" in an official capacity.

A Servant Ministry to the People and the Elders

Everyone is called to become a follower, a disciple. Everyone is called to serve. A deacon is called to be a servant in an official office of service. The idea for the office came from the concept of service. We find a rapidly growing church described in the book of Acts. A transition seems to take place somewhere between Acts chapters 2 and 6 as the church grew, increasing the work of serving. The elders had become burdened with the task of seeing to the needs of families who were being ignored in the distribution of food. In Acts 6:1-6 the apostles, who later referred to themselves as elders, give instructions for the church to identify seven people who met certain qualifications. When they had been identified, the apostles appointed the seven to the work of service in order to be free themselves to spend time in the all important ministry of the Word of God, which is a ministry specifically delegated to elders. Whether we accept the assumption that the office of deacon was created here or not, we can conclude that the deacon is involved in a "ministry of service." Deacons provide help in support and maintenance of the organization, which includes freeing the elders to accomplish their roles, managing facilities, and caring for the members of the flock, all while working alongside the elders.

Believers who exhibit appropriate maturity and character qualifications may be appointed to the leadership position represented by the deacon. The deacon is to be like the elder in many respects, but is never referred to as "overseer" or "shepherd." The elders' authority is exercised through the teaching of Scripture. Deacons serve in cooperation and under the supervision of the elders. Since both Scripture and historical documents point to these offices being coordinated, we should strive to link them together in like manner in our churches as well.

Today we have adopted the use of many terms referring to people who are not elders or pastors but have been placed in a variety of ministries and church leadership positions. In our culture, we seem obsessed with titles. We often use terms like "Church board," "Deacon board," "Board of Directors," "Committee chairperson," "Under shepherd," "Small group leader," "Youth leader," "Sunday school teacher," and "Minister of 'whatever'". People being what they are, titles often go to their heads, resulting in a response of control or authority that the Bible may never have intended to give. This response may well come from a desire to "Lord it over" caused by sin.

I suggest the Bible uses only three general terms to describe the people who make up the flock of God: saints (members), elders, and deacons, all of whom have made the decision to become a disciple of Christ. Everyone is called to be a disciple and to serve one another. Identification with Christ is the first step to becoming a member of the flock, and this is how one becomes a "saint." Discipleship is the qualification of one who commits to obey Christ as a member of His flock. There are also qualifications for becoming elders and deacons, who are selected from the more mature saints to serve in their positions.

Call me simple minded if you like, but my early business training taught me, "Keep it simple, salesman." I love it when churches are clear in their understanding and description of the various leadership positions occupied by their people, but especially when they are clear regarding their members, elders, and deacons, as well as clear on what it means to be a disciple. The reality is that we need to use terms to refer to the things people do in church today, and these terms should be culturally relevant to the people we are trying to reach. I am okay with that. We just need to be careful to have a clear Biblical understanding of what we mean as we apply those terms, regardless of the ones we choose to use. A few cautions are in order. Be especially careful about accountability and the delegation of authority when using titles. Don't use titles as a means of giving or taking authority inappropriately. Follow the Biblical chain of command. Submit to leaders. Serve one another in an environment that cares for people and values the development of people toward maturity. The culture among your top leaders will set the stage for everything else that happens. If there is a stressful, disagreeable environment causing high turnover among your leaders and staff, something is dreadfully wrong at the top. Paul writes, *"And now these three remain: faith, hope and love. But the greatest of these is love"* (1Cor 13:13). Loving relationships become the evidence of an effective leadership model.

Under the general heading of "deacon," we may find a whole variety of ministries requiring the accomplishment of all kinds of tasks. Perhaps your church refers to them as a Deacon Board or a Board of Directors.

Whatever name is used, the job requires Biblically qualified people for the position. Organizing people into any sense of order is facilitated by using terms to refer to their position and/or rank. It becomes confusing when a person occupies a position and has the idea that they are in authority over everyone else, including elders. Being a "deacon board member" or "team leader" or "ministry leader" or "small group leader" does not convey authority higher than that of elder. I would also suggest that just because a person joins the church, he or she is not necessarily ready to lead, especially if they are a new believer.

After salvation is received, the biblical expectation is for a believer to become a disciple and start down the path to maturity, a path that helps them learn to live a full Christ centered life. Then, their skill at "serving" or "speaking" can be identified, and they can be put to work. Over time, they should be given a chance to lead. But, don't be hasty lest you run the risk of putting the blind in charge of leading the blind! Training comes before leading.

> ***Luke 6:39-40*** *He also told them this parable: "Can a blind man lead a blind man? Will they not both fall into a pit? A student is not above his teacher, but everyone who is fully trained will be like his teacher.*

This passage is found within a teaching that begins at Luke 6:17 and ends at Luke 6:49. The lesson plan of this passage, when taken in context, is to teach us about blessings and woes, loving and judging, leading and following, producing good fruit, and being a wise builder. The truth is that a disciple is expected to learn how to judge good from bad and right from wrong through understanding and applying God's Word. In Luke 6, the word "student" comes from the same word Jesus spoke when giving us the Great Commission, there translated "disciple." The implication is that people are not capable of leading others toward Christian maturity and discipleship until they have received training as students of the Word. It is only possible to make good judgments when they are based on the Word of God. Some may claim that we can identify when a brother or sister is engaged in unchristian or unrighteous behavior. But we cannot do so without knowledge of God and direction from Scripture. When armed with this knowledge, we can make good judgments, we can help our brother remove the speck from his eye, and we can produce good fruit. Leadership positions within the church should be filled only with people who are making progress in this area. Otherwise the church ends up with the blind leading the blind, which leads everyone into a pit.

Technically, and according to terms used in Scripture, anyone who serves the church in any recognized position other than elder is generally a deacon, regardless of the title you may assign. Everyone else is a member, called "saint," and is hopefully committed to being a disciple.

The following table should help picture the relationship between these two general offices as together they serve to train the people and coordinate all the work of ministry, so that the mission of Christ may be accomplished by all.

TABLE 13: Elder and Deacon Board Illustration

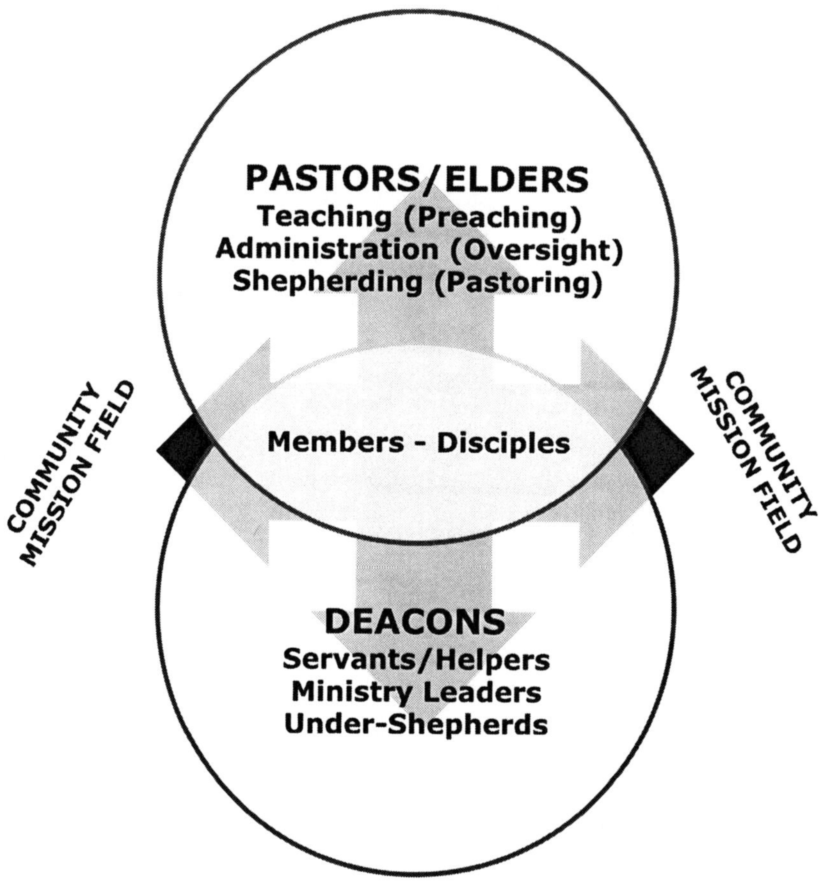

Everyone is responsible to evangelize among the lost in their community by sharing their faith with others. As people repent and become members of the church, they need to be taught and trained how to be disciples. It is my opinion that the mission of the church is to make disciples, and for elders to equip the saints to do the work of service. The way in which we do life together as members of the church should result in people coming to Christ for salvation. Many tasks need to be accomplished within the church. Mature disciples who are known to exhibit the required character qualifications should be selected to serve in various ministries of service.

Some will have management and leadership responsibility for various service ministries. They may be called deacons or given other titles, and they should receive direction from the elders while cooperating with them. The ministry of the Word of God must be the priority of the church because people will only be changed by His Word, not our word. Real change cannot happen in someone who is not engaged with the Word of God and its life changing message while doing life together with other disciples in loving relationships. We cannot repent and follow Jesus by acting only on our feelings about how to live correctly. In sum, the lines of authority go from Scripture to elders to deacons and to members, and everyone is led down a path that follows after Jesus.

Members who grow and mature in their understanding and faith will serve with greater responsibility over time. Some will become deacons, servants in the formal sense of the word, and be assigned to various leadership positions. Some will become pastors. Many will be active members, serving in and among the body of believers. The teamwork, loving relationships, cooperation, and service represented by the entire body as they work together should be obvious to everyone who sees the church in action, sticking out like a sore thumb in this land that is not our true home.

A good organizational structure is critical to achieving the purpose of the church. I submit this structure has been well illustrated in God's Word. Why is it so difficult to comply with it? Could it have something to do with loving relationships and obedience, or the lack thereof?

CHAPTER 7

A culture that values the development of people will make disciples who become leaders who make disciples.

Jim Kirkland

Coaching People to Grow

The key to success in achieving the fivefold purpose of the church lies in the development of people. We should place a high value on helping people grow in maturity and in relationship with others. We need a culture that encourages believers to be disciples, who in turn become leaders who make disciples. Guiding people through the process of accepting Christ for salvation, falling in love with God, changing how they live, and learning to share the good news with others requires coaching and mentoring. Mature believers are in love with the idea of helping people know their best friend, Jesus. I like to describe the evangelism process this way: make a friend, be a friend, and win that friend to Christ. After that, mentoring them toward authentic Christian living should be the goal.

We should be very careful and even deliberate about eliminating barriers that may hinder a person from encountering Jesus. We the "churched" tend to use jargon and images in a way that create barriers to the "un-churched" and make them very uncomfortable. The Apostle Paul said, *"Be careful, however, that the exercise of your freedom does not become a stumbling block to the weak" (1 Corinthians 8:7).* I believe this instruction applies not just to food choices and addictions but to everything we do. Listen to what else Paul says:

> *Though I am free and belong to no man, I make myself a slave to everyone, to win as many as possible. To the Jews I became like a Jew,*

> *to win the Jews. To those under the law I became like one under the law (though I myself am not under the law), so as to win those under the law. To those not having the law I became like one not having the law (though I am not free from God's law but am under Christ's law), so as to win those not having the law. To the weak I became weak, to win the weak. I have become all things to all men so that by all possible means I might save some. I do all this for the sake of the gospel, that I may share in its blessings" (1 Corinthians 9:19-23).*

"So that by all possible means we might save some!" My conclusion is that as we reach out to the community we should be very careful not to let anything get in the way of evangelism. The sad truth is that we live in a new reality, a world influenced by New Age and postmodern thought. These have had a profound influence on our culture. Terms that we take for granted, like "Evangelical Christian" or "Way of the Cross," have been re-defined by the culture to mean something very negative. This change in meaning has happened right under our noses, yet we persist in using terms that may be an impediment to many. The church has largely become entrenched and self focused in response to this new reality. Instead of figuring out how to repackage the message in a way that will reach the people who are lost, we become a holy huddle that creates a barrier that discourages the unsaved from wanting what we have. Rather than argue over church jargon and its meaning, learn to present the Gospel in relevant ways.

The important thing is in pointing people to Jesus as the only way to heaven. People matter most to God so we need to step out of our comfort zone in order to make them feel comfortable enough to check us out. Remember, it is not about "Me," but rather "God and His people!" We need to be careful how we accomplish this however. One dear pastor friend of mine explains it this way, *"I believe there are many well intentioned churches that have reacted to this new reality by trying to reform the church around the surrounding culture when they should be figuring out how to reform the culture around the church."*

The church should have a process for moving people from community to visitor, visitor to attender, attender to member, member to disciple, and disciple to leader. On one side of the decision for Christ is our presentation of the Gospel by how we live among them. I would add that the way we "do church" should recognize this. On the other side of the decision is the presentation of the Gospel by how we teach sound doctrine, with the expectation of gradually increasing maturity toward Christ over time. There needs to be a "handoff" from the front end of evangelism to the back end of discipleship.

Coaching people toward growth in the Christian life is a "big picture" idea, and it is the responsibility of leadership to make it a primary focus. The church needs to have a culture that highly values the development of people toward a changed life and increasing maturity in Christ. It may take time to change the culture. Growth is often a slow process that takes many months, even years, before getting noticed. While we are living here in our temporary quarters, the focus should be on sharing Christ and helping believers grow. That is what a leader does. A good coach encourages growth in maturity and trusts God for the increase. There are many church leaders today who have this reversed and the church is suffering for it.

Growth is Expected in Scripture

The Scripture expects growth. Jesus taught about growth in several passages of Scripture. Matthew chapter 25 provides an excellent example. The Kingdom of Heaven is like a person who discovers something of great value and tells everyone about it. The discovery becomes the most important thing in the person's life. Perhaps the most well known teaching about growth is the parable of the talents (Matthew 25: 14-30). In this passage Jesus explains that the Kingdom of Heaven is like something that grows out of our commitment to what is most important to us. He compares and contrasts disciples who saw the value of the gift of Christ with one who did not.

As you review this passage, focus on the poor soul who buried the talent in the ground because he thought the Lord was a hard task master. It is difficult to serve someone you do not love, in a relationship you do not value. If the gift is not valued, the request to serve the giver will feel more like slavery. Think about this person for a moment. He did not value the gift He was given. He did not love God above all else. This person was dead in His sin and did not value the great freedom offered in Christ. He buried the talent in the same place where they put dead bodies. He rejected the gift because it would not allow him to do whatever he wanted.

The most important thing to this fellow was himself. From the time he received the gift to the time the master returned for an accounting, he was busy living his life – his way. He was busily working to bring an increase in the things that mattered to him, just like many of us. It isn't that he sat back and did nothing; otherwise he would have starved to death! No, he disregarded the gift of Christ because he was more in love with himself and his own desires than God and His will. The very idea that Christ wanted him to bring an increase in what matters most to God was repulsive. It was repulsive because of the expectation that he should desire something outside himself. This parable shows us what a person is like who says, "I am a Christian," but does not really value God more than himself and has not changed his mind about what is really important. He does not value the gift of Christ because the focus is "selfish" rather than "selfless."

It should be fairly obvious when people do not truly love God, in spite of their claim to be "Christians." True followers of Jesus will value the gift of grace more than anything else in life. They will live in a way that demonstrates their love of God and His people, telling everyone about the treasure they have received. They will live in service to others, resulting in an increase in what matters most to God: an increase in the quality of the relationships a believer has through Christ, and in the number of people whose lives are restored through Christ. God wants fruit to be produced in the people who call Him "Father" and have a relationship with Him. He also wants an increase in spiritual maturity and knowledge of Him. How can we follow Him if we do not know His ways? Moses had it right when he said to the Lord, *"If you are pleased with me, teach me your ways so I may know you and continue to find favor with you" (Exodus 33:13).* The man in the parable Jesus called a "worthless servant" was ultimately proven to be something other than His follower and was thrown out of the Kingdom, into a place where there is much sorrow. We should be serious about helping people avoid going to this place, at all cost!

Growth Requires Change

Growth is a continual process for all believers. One who does not love God does not grow. All believers should grow in several areas because of their love for God and each other. Growth in knowledge of God should change how we think and live. Growth should increase our spiritual maturity and faith. Growth should influence our relationship with others. In all of this there should be progress toward maturity and leadership, showing others how to follow Christ and why they should want to do so. The areas where Scripture expects growth and change can be listed:

- Change in thinking (Repentance)
- Change in living (Visible difference fueled by a Love of God)
- Increasing faith (Trusting God)
- Increasing maturity (Learning and applying the Word of God)
- Loving relationships (Loving others-increase in community)
- Progress in following Christ (Joyful Obedience)
- Progress toward leadership (Discipleship)

A change in <u>thinking</u> is expected. After a person becomes a believer, they should experience a change of mind. Scripture uses the word "repent." Such a change happens through the renewing of your mind by application of the Word of God. We are encouraged to no longer conform to the pattern of thinking as taught by the world, but rather to learn how to know the good and pleasing and perfect will of God (Romans 12:2). This can only be accomplished through the Word of God, since His word changes minds and our words only cause disagreement.

A change in <u>living</u> is expected. The result of a change in thinking is a changed life. A follower of Jesus does not blend in with the rest of the culture. We should stand out. Scripture uses the word "holy" or "set apart for the purpose of God" to describe the believer. As we fall ever deeper in love with God and His people, how we live will be noticeably different. This change may take time, but it should be evident in the life of a follower of Christ. We should simply be different as a result of our salvation. Are we multiplying the gift we received or burying it in the ground? Is your church serious about showing people how to live for Christ?

An increase in <u>faith</u> is expected. Our faith is demonstrated by how we act and by what we do. The letter of James is all about faith that perseveres and changes lives. Many of us have experienced hardship and loss that is difficult to cope with. We have desires that we hope God will provide to us. When we are faced with hardship, or loss, or persecution, the circumstances may cause us to feel a need to cry out to God, asking: "Why God, why?" In these dark and difficult times God answers our question with one of His own, saying, "Do you trust me?" When God is our focus, it becomes a little easier to trust him even when things are not going our way. We can experience joy in living, even during the darkest of times, when our faith in God is solid. This faith should be growing as we learn that God is God and we are not. He loves us enough to die for us, so why on earth is it so difficult to trust Him? Since He knows everything, does He not also know the desires of our heart? Does He not also know what is best for us in the long run? Does He not see the future and how to use our trials to bring others into a relationship with Him or bring about a change He desires to make? We need to have faith in Him and learn to trust Him, no matter what. Such faith does not happen by accident, but through training.

An increase in maturity is expected. We grow in maturity through several means. We grow as we learn God's Word and apply it to our lives. We grow as we learn to trust the guiding hand of the Holy Spirit living inside us. We grow as we become involved in relationships with other believers who are also learning to walk the walk we talk. In our growing maturity the way we act and speak and live and love will change. We use loving language more and foul language less. We sacrifice our desires in favor of helping others. We become involved with serving in ministry with others. Our desire to please God increases. We are less concerned with conforming to the pattern of this world and more concerned with living for Christ. We learn to value God first - me last, and we experience joy in increasing measure as we do.

Growth in loving relationships is expected. Believers love God and people. They should increasingly desire to participate in life with other believers. We need to encourage new believers to get plugged in and involved with others. They should be invited to participate with fellow believers who are really interested in living their faith by doing life together for Christ. We accomplish this best in ministry teams and small groups. It is really easy for people to hide in the crowd. Don't let them. Over time, more and more people should become involved in ministry and be serious about building life long relationships with others. More than anywhere else, this model of loving relationships will be modeled among your top leaders and bring growth or it will not be modeled with resulting stress and turnover among your people.

Progress toward <u>leadership</u> is expected. Frankly, the only way leadership can be successful is by duplication. The disciple-making process is not one of simple addition but rather one of multiplication. The end result of effective mentoring, caring and coaching is to bring more people into leadership. By doing so, we dramatically increase the number of people whose lives are impacted for Christ. In a church where 100 mature leaders duplicate themselves, suddenly the 100 leaders become 200 leaders. These will become 400. Four hundred become 800 and so on! Everyone is expected to grow in Christian maturity. Everyone should have at least some influence on someone else for Christ. Living for Him as empowered by the Holy Spirit has an impact. Otherwise, we are no different than the poor fellow who buried his talent in the ground. What is our focus? All of us should be encouraging people toward discipleship, and many more people should be joining the ranks of leadership over time. This is how disciples are multiplied, and this is also how involvement in ministry and small groups will be increased.

Success in increasing the involvement of your people in ministry teams and small groups depends on the culture of your church. It will take time to create a culture that places a high value on developing people. Consider making an honest assessment of your church to determine if you are making progress in developing people. Changing your culture to achieve better results will probably take between three and five years. The change must first take place at the top and filter its way down. It is like a little yeast in the dough. Eventually it will work its way through the entire batch. Don't expect to create a great process and suddenly achieve dramatic results. The culture needs to change first, and change takes time. Several obstacles get in the way of a cultural shift that values the development of people.

Obstacles to Growth

- Failure to empower others to lead

If we fail to encourage maturing believers to get involved in leadership, we will fail to achieve healthy growth. Sometimes it is difficult to pass the baton of leadership to someone else. This may be due to our ego getting in the way. Maybe we fear they won't do the job as well as we would. Maybe we fear for our job security if someone else seems more capable. Maybe we don't relate to the way someone else gets something done. Many possible reasons for this failure are possible, but the question remains, "Do I hold onto control and fail to empower mature believers to lead?" The truth is that God has made many different types of people, each with his or her own unique SHAPE. If leadership in your church attempts to control the work of the Holy Spirit by using a cookie cutter that forces everyone into the same shape, the church will fail to empower good people to participate in ministry.

Another failure is in handing leadership to a person who is not qualified or ready to lead. I have seen churches that put people in charge of a ministry simply because they volunteered. Immature believers can lead people down a wrong path. They should be engaged in learning the Word of God and get plugged into a small group or ministry team where they will learn how to live more like Jesus by following others who are also learning to live like Jesus. Take time to assess their maturity and growth. Consider their knowledge of Scripture and progress toward genuine discipleship. Observe how they are functioning among members of the body. Of course, we cannot expect perfection. After all, Christ does not require it! But we should be sure to help people grow before placing them into leadership. In Scripture, training comes before leading. The blind cannot lead the blind (Luke 6:39)!

- Failure to make disciples who also become leaders

The church has largely lost the art of making disciples. For many, church has become a replacement for the local country club. It is where we go to be involved with friends, have a nice cup of coffee and enjoy some fellowship. It is a great place to find something to do and feel good about ourselves. In truth, the process of guiding people along a path of discipleship should lead everyone toward maturity and many into leadership. A mature Christian will help others toward salvation and discipleship. This progression of maturity is not only logical, but is the command of Jesus: *"Make disciples."* Since this is part of our purpose, we need to make it a priority without letting the process become a barrier to Christ.

- Failure to have an intentional process

Many churches understand the importance of making disciples but fail to have a process for achieving it. Again, the culture itself must expect it. When everyone in leadership values it, a process to achieve it can be developed far more easily. As with all relationships from the time we are young, peer pressure works! Folks should be led along a path from attending, to salvation and membership, to discipleship, and eventually to leadership. Every organization has a culture that places subliminal pressure on its members to do certain things. Sometimes this peer pressure can lead to bad things, sometimes good. It is important for you to make an honest assessment of the fruit being produced in your church. In general, would you describe it as good fruit or bad fruit? How do you know? Are loving relationships evident? Disciples made? Are people coming to Christ? Our culture should employ peer pressure that gently encourages people to make progress toward change. This is a good thing!

We need to be careful not to make programs our focus. Programs by themselves will not achieve the mission. They will keep a lot of people busy, sometimes too busy but to what end? It is not about the things we do; it is about the care and development of people toward health and maturity. I think we tend to create too many programs without paying attention to developing a culture that expects real growth. Again, we must seek growth in knowledge, love, and relationships as we accomplish ministry together. Many churches would improve by doing fewer things really well and with the right focus, rather than many things poorly with the wrong one. The ultimate test is in the relationships your people have with each other and the growth being produced as the function together.

- Spiritual and Biblical illiteracy

People should be trained in Scripture and in how to think Biblically. The folks we are trying to reach today are skeptical of the Bible and need to be shown that it really is the Word of God. It is impossible for us to grow in righteous living apart from God. He gave us instructions that will change our lives, but unchurched people are intimidated by it. As a consequence, we need to make the Bible a priority at every level and present it as friendly and in a friendly way! The way we change our minds is through the study and application of God's Word. This process is facilitated by the Holy Spirit growing in our lives. Most importantly, our growth in this area is best accomplished while in relationship with other believers. Have you defined a learning process for your people, a process that works? Are your people engaged with the Word of God?

- A shortage of leaders

A culture that does not value the development of people will not be successful in developing disciples or effective leaders. A culture that does not develop leaders will not achieve healthy growth. I believe this is what Jesus was talking about when He had compassion on the large crowds of people seeking him out for help. He said to His disciples, *"The harvest is plentiful but the workers are few" (Matthew 9:37)*. Far too many people need guidance to be shepherded well by just a handful of leaders. How many folks can one person effectively shepherd? Mature workers and leaders are a very important commodity, and there is a real shortage of them. Does your church have a leadership vacuum and high turnover? Why?

Breakthroughs Happen in Smaller Groups of People

It is not possible to have meaningful relationships with hundreds or thousands of people. We can only really know small numbers of people. Our ability to grow in spiritual maturity is greatly enhanced when we are involved in doing life with others, focused on living for Christ. It is in participation with mature believers, small groups and ministry teams that "Aha" moments will happen. In a growing church, it becomes easy for an individual to hide among the crowd of people. Yet, a person's ability to grow is enhanced when he or she can be in relationship with other more mature believers. Our culture should apply the necessary peer pressure to encourage involvement in such relationships. Since most people will be more comfortable hiding, we should encourage our leaders to seek them out and invite them to participate. Often we make an announcement saying, "We have posted a list of small groups getting started and encourage you to join one." Then, we leave it up to the interested people to make the first contact, but most of them will not. Most people will, however, come to your home for dinner or dessert if they are invited to do so! In fact, it was this kind of personal invitation that led my wife and I to salvation and discipleship.

Others who may not be ready for the small group experience may be comfortable attending a larger gathering to learn about something they are interested in. Create an environment that gradually connects people with smaller and more intimate groups of people where a healthy relationship can be built. Many people are interested in learning about their new faith but uncomfortable jumping in with a group of strangers. Frankly, this really does weird some people out. Don't force it, but create an environment that encourages it. Engage in a process that casts several different kinds of nets into the crowd, each one encouraging movement toward the small group or house church model.

One example of a possible net or way to accomplish this is to create various presentations on specific topics designed for groups of fifty to a hundred. The material should be taught over a four to six week period of time. This is a short enough timeframe to be non-threatening. Most people will say, "I am okay with a short term commitment like this, where I can still feel safe in the crowd while I am checking things out." When they come, assign them to a specific table with a mature believer or couple who will serve as that table's small group leader for the series. At the end of the series, have another one ready to go on a different subject that builds on the one just completed. Eventually, as relationships are built, the table leaders can invite their new friends over for dessert and fellowship. Voila, a small group is born.

We Need More Leaders

Paul instructed Timothy to pass on leadership, and we should take heed of his message.

> *And the things you have heard me say in the presence of many witnesses entrust to reliable men who will also be qualified to teach others (2 Timothy 2:2).*

The Pauline Ministry Cycle

We can observe the process used by the Apostle Paul by reading through chapter 14 of Acts. The following chart helps to picture the process that moved seekers through maturity and into leadership:

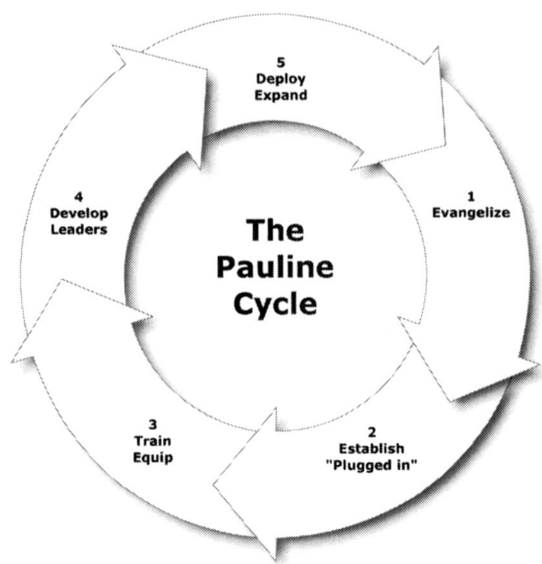

Paul started every new relationship with evangelism. He shared the good news with everyone he met. As people accepted the truth of the gospel, they became involved in relationships with other believers. A small house church was established. Together, they learned from the Word of God how to live for Christ. They were trained and equipped for ministry. Over time, people who were maturing in their faith began to share it with others. As we observe mature believers functioning among the body of believers, we see them getting involved in leadership. They began to serve in ministry to others. Some were selected to be deacons; some became elders. Leaders were deployed and empowered for ministry. The church expanded as more people joined. The process continued, and exponential growth was experienced. We need more leaders, or we will fail.

The people involved in the churches established by Paul led a lifestyle of discipleship. They were in relationship with each other as they did life together for Christ. The gift of Christ was so important to them that it became the focus of their lives. They loved God and each other and it showed. As a result, God added to their number and the process of leadership development continued. When they got off track, Paul provided instruction to bring them back to the center.

Return to the Center where People Matter Most

The center of church life is people. People, more than anything, matter to God. We need to return to the center and focus more on the development of people. Our work is about the body, not the building. Programs are important, but not as important as people. Any program or process we develop should always have the mission and purpose of the church in mind. We should always ask, "If we implement this program, will it achieve our primary goal of developing people?" If not, don't add the program. Everything should revolve around the most important thing. Return to the center. Proper love and care for the people you have will eventually result in an increase of new people attending your church.

Training Ground for Leaders

I believe the best training ground for leaders is in mentoring relationships, small groups, or ministry teams, coupled with opportunity for learning from the Word of God. Existing leaders should be encouraged to think as shepherd leaders. They should be observing the members of their group and identify those who are maturing. These folks should be groomed for leadership, and, at some point, encouraged to lead a small group of their own. A small group that stays together year after year, never spinning off other groups or encouraging others to join them does not work. This type of small group has become, in reality, a small church or holy huddle that values its traditions more than the mission. I fear that a group such as this is in danger of burying their talent in the ground.

Our structure should encourage everyone to grow in maturity and many to become leaders. Some folks will be leaders of a small number of people. Others will become leaders of leaders. The result is a process that helps people become leaders who train leaders who make disciples. It is the same process used by the Apostle Paul, and it will work in your church!

A Process to Develop People

A culture that values the development of people will have a process or path that accomplishes that aim. In general, we start with evangelism and make progress toward discipleship. Throughout the process we should be careful to teach sound doctrine, but in ways that don't hinder the Gospel from being received by the culture we are trying to reach.

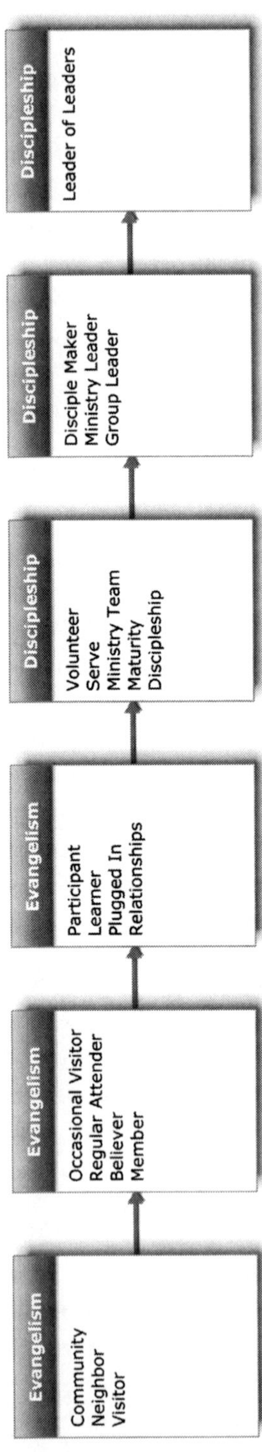
People Development Path
Evangelism
Community
Neighbor
Visitor
Evangelism
Occasional Visitor
Regular Attender
Believer
Member
Evangelism
Participant
Learner
Plugged In
Relationships
Discipleship
Volunteer
Serve
Ministry Team
Maturity
Discipleship
Discipleship
Disciple Maker
Ministry Leader
Group Leader
Discipleship
Leader of Leaders

I like to think of the process as a front wheel and a back wheel, like on a bicycle. The front wheel would represent evangelism and the back wheel discipleship. Leadership drives the bike forward under guidance from the Holy Spirit and Word of God. The direction is determined by vision and purpose, which is affected greatly by the church's culture.

The front wheel should be focused on reaching the lost in culturally relevant ways. Nothing should hinder the message we have to share. Don't be afraid to move forward in ways that are unfamiliar to you, because we need to figure out how to become familiar to those outside the church. Reaching the lost in ways comfortable for them does not mean watering down the Gospel message. It simply means showing them the Gospel by how we live and act and talk and serve. An old saying may sum it up best: "You may be the only Bible a person ever sees." Live it out to the best of your ability and share Christ with others.

At some point in time after a person has become a believer and joined your church, there should be a transition to discipleship. The study and application of Scripture is very important to spiritual maturity. We need to teach sound doctrine while proclaiming the Good News of Christ. Traditional classroom teaching is fine and may work in your church as long as you are successful at getting high participation from your members. If participation is low, be willing to be creative in this area. However, my experience is that people really do hunger for the word of God and if you teach it, they will come.

You may need to reach your people in different ways while teaching the clear message of the Bible. It is a priority for discipleship. The ministry of the Word of God should be the most important thing. There is no other way to learn how to obey the commands of Christ than from the instruction He provided, and it is required of anyone who aspires to a life lived well for Christ. Help the members understand what we believe and why we believe it. Encourage them to trust God's Word and learn to read it themselves.

CHAPTER 8

I love to hear a choir. I love the humanity... to see the faces of real people devoting themselves to a piece of music. I like the teamwork. It makes me feel optimistic about the human race when I see them cooperating like that.

- Paul McCartney[94]

Together Everyone Achieves More!

TEAM

T = Together

E = Everyone

A = Achieves

M = More

Teamwork makes the mission actually work!

From the mouth of a non-Christian we find words of wisdom regarding the impact of Christian teamwork: "I like the teamwork. It makes me feel optimistic..." When Christian people do life together as Scripture describes it, wonderful things happen and miracles take place. Such a people will be different. They will stand out and offer hope to a dying world because of the visible difference in how they function with each other in love. The Gospel of Jesus Christ is most certainly "Good News." People who see us working together should be filled with a sense of optimism and hope.

Key words that would describe a body of believers who are working well as a team may include love, obedience, dedication, submission, serving, learning, giving, sharing, joy, excellence, patience, peace, kindness, self control, humble, and generous. We can form a word picture out of them that describes the expectation Christ has of a people calling themselves "The Church." Such a team of people will stand out from the rest of the world and they will be noticed. Their effectiveness will be evident as they work together to accomplish the mission and purpose we have been given by Christ himself.

A summary of the purpose and mission of the church:

1. **Love God**: We make him first in everything. Love Him with all of our heart, soul, mind and strength. Everything else flows out of this application of "worth" as we "worship" Him.

2. **Love others**: We love our neighbors with a new heart because of what He has done for us and because the Holy Spirit is at work in us. Place God first, people next, and ourselves last. This love of others should be most evident among your church staff and leadership team.

3. **Evangelism**: We share our faith with others as we live a life focused on "going" and "making" followers of Jesus – disciples.

4. **Identification**: In this part, a person accepts Christ for salvation and makes a commitment to repent, take up their cross, and follow. We die to ourselves while being raised to a new life in Christ, a new way of living - represented by baptism.

5. **Discipleship**: We become dedicated students of the Word of God so that we can learn how to follow and obey Him. We live in loving relationships as we help each other walk the walk we talk.

Primary Job Description of a Member

A disciple is focused on following Christ and living to achieve the purpose He has given us. Our primary job description as a member of God's house is to be a disciple while doing our part in helping others become disciples also. Discipleship implies a change in living through spiritual growth as we learn to follow Jesus. This happens through the renewing of our mind. This kind of growth can only be achieved by applying God's Word in our lives. We need the help of the Holy Spirit while living in relationship and community with fellow believers. We can only apply His Word if we read it and have help from the Holy Spirit living in us. Growth in our character and righteousness is best accomplished by doing life together, committed to loving relationships as we share Christ's love with each other. The Scripture explains it best, while admonishing all of us to serve well in spite of our differences.

> *"Therefore, I urge you, brothers, in view of God's mercy, to offer your bodies as living sacrifices, holy and pleasing to God-- this is your spiritual act of worship. Do not conform any longer to the pattern of this world, but be transformed by the renewing of your mind. Then you will be able to test and approve what God's will is-- his good, pleasing and perfect will. For by the grace given me I say to every one of you: Do not think of yourself more highly than you ought, but rather think of yourself with sober judgment, in accordance with the measure of faith God has given you. Just as each of us has one body with many members, and these members do not all have the same function, so in Christ we who are many form one body, and each member belongs to all the others"* (Romans 12:1-5).

The balance of chapter 12 provides a beautiful description of God's people living together in loving relationships, in a community that honors each person's unique gifts and abilities. From the first five verses of this chapter we can make note of several points that help us understand the job description of a member, called a "saint" (see Rom 1:7, 2Cor 1:1 and Eph 1:1):

- Offer your whole self as an act of worship, a life of service;
- Take your focus off the world, its desires, and its way of doing things;
- Be transformed by the renewal of your mind (study and apply the Word);
- Learn to discern between the way of the world and God's way, and follow His;
- Do not be haughty, interested in power and position over others (serve others);
- Everyone has different gifts, abilities, and a function that is different from everyone else;

- In Christ we are part of one body and each one of us belongs to everyone else as we are fitted into relationships and serve Christ together.

Each of us has different gifts to use in accomplishing the mission. Yet, it is only when we are fit together with other believers that ministry can be truly accomplished. You will reach people with your story and your gifts that I would never be able to reach, and vice versa. You contribute a variety of gifts and talents that are unique to you alone. You will be capable of doing a job well that I could not do poorly on a good day. When God first thought you up, He already had in mind a job for you to do: a job that you alone are designed to accomplish.

Team Building Based on Gifts and Temperament

Scripture tells us about a variety of spiritual gifts, given to each believer in varying degrees. Some people are highly gifted with leadership, others with teaching, mercy, helping and so on. Peter suggests the existence of two general or special gifts given to the people of God. They are general categories out of which flow all other spiritual gifts provided in varying mixes to every believer. He describes the general categories as "the gift of serving" and "the gift of speaking."

> *"As each one has received a special gift, employ it in serving one another as good stewards of the manifold grace of God. Whoever speaks, is to do so as one who is speaking the utterances of God; whoever serves is to do so as one who is serving by the strength which God supplies; so that in all things God may be glorified through Jesus Christ, to whom belongs the glory and dominion forever and ever. Amen"* (NASB 1 Peter 4:10-11.)

Both "serving" and "speaking" are important, but they are not the same. They do not accomplish the same jobs, nor do they carry the same degree or type of authority. Everyone is called to serve and help in a general sense, for the very nature of Christianity is one of service. But not everyone is called to speak and lead. My wife will jump in to help a group of folks clean the church kitchen out of the sheer joy of helping others complete a task in fellowship with each other. She experiences joy in helping, joy in completing tasks on a checklist. But please don't ask her to stand up in front of a group to make an announcement or give a talk or make a bunch of phone calls! She might pass out. On the other hand, I love mentoring, planning, preaching and teaching. I will spend hours preparing a talk and simply love watching the impact of its delivery on the faces of people who learn from God's Word. I love training people for a job while mentoring them in spiritual growth, watching them make progress toward reaching a goal. I love managing people and keeping them focused on the big picture, but I really don't like helping with tasks very much. Together, my wife and I make a very good team. It should be like this among your elders/pastors and deacons, as well as with every member and ministry team your church puts together for any purpose.

The Lord gave to each a special gift which made some to be ***servers*** and others to be ***speakers***, with everyone dedicated to pleasing Him. Everyone is gifted with a little of each, but which one is your primary strength? Are you designed to be a server, a helper? Or are you designed to be a speaker, a leader? Where do you best fit as a member of the team? Everyone is called to serve, but not everyone is called to lead. Not all who are called to lead are also called to be an elder/pastor.

Numerous specific gifts have been given at the will and discretion of the Holy Spirit. Everyone has a unique personality and temperament. Everyone has a set of gifts that are unique from everyone else. Have you identified your own unique mixture of talents, spiritual gifts, experience, temperament and abilities? Do you know your SHAPE? The moment you become responsible to lead others, you have become a manager. To manage well, you need to be in relationship with them and know them. Elders/pastors need to get a handle on this idea of teamwork because their primary job requires an ability to achieve ministry through people. They need first to demonstrate effective teamwork and loving relationships among themselves, dividing the work of managing (oversight), preaching (teaching) and shepherding (pastoring) according to their own spiritual gifts and abilities. A good place to start is to identify your strengths and weaknesses. This will help to identify the people you need on your team who will take up the slack in areas where you may be lacking. Be careful here not to allow these Holy Spirit inspired differences to become a source of friction or disagreement. God created each of us to be different so don't make the mistake of trying to put together a team based on a culture of sameness. This is the essence of building a good team. It makes no sense whatsoever to have a team made up of people who have all the same gifts and abilities and attitudes.

Some Help from Behavioral Science

Some help is available to you through the field of behavioral science and spiritual gift analysis. The entire concept of behavioral science is from a very old teaching. Quite a number of personality and spiritual gift assessment tools are available, and I recommend putting them to good use. Though many would have you believe their temperament system is proprietary and unique, one look at any particular approach and you will see its similarity to the 2400 year old theory of "Hippocrates," who observed four basic human temperaments in two main categories: Extroverted people called "Sanguine" and "Choleric" and Introverted people called "Melancholy" and "Phlegmatic."[95]

An extrovert is outgoing, people oriented, and prone to "speak or tell." An introvert is task oriented and prone to "serve or help." This early temperament theory was prevalent among the thinkers of Peter's day, and I wonder if he was familiar with it. 1 Peter 4:10-11 seems to be making the obvious point that some folks are people oriented "speakers" and others are task oriented "servants." One is admonished to speak as with the very words of God, while the other is asked to serve with all the strength God provides. The purpose of these two general categories of gifts is so that in all things God is glorified through Christ. We are each part of the Body of Christ, each member given a special function and job to accomplish. This is so cool it gives me goosebumps!

If we are to achieve the mission of the church, the fivefold purpose given by Christ, we need to learn how to work well with each other. It is in our loving relationships that ministry will be effective. It is in our love for God and each other that we will become an effective organization, one that looks different from the world. God will bring success when we follow a Biblical structure that allows us to serve well together. We have seen that the elder/pastor has the primary job description of "equipping the saints." Since management is one of the key responsibilities of the elder/pastor, it follows that we need to learn how to work well with people and place them on our team in a way that improves the effectiveness of ministry. I am a proponent of getting to know people well enough to know how to equip them so that we can send them out to accomplish the mission. Temperament theory and assessment tools can be very helpful in developing the kind of Biblical teamwork needed to accomplish it.

Three categories of People in the Church

"Elders and Deacons and Saints, Oh My!"

Generally the term "member" refers to anyone who has professed belief in Jesus for their salvation, been baptized, and joined a church. Jesus asks everyone who is a member to become His "disciple" and all that the word implies. Every member can be described by one of three Biblical words: saint, elder or deacon. Leading people into the kind of working relationship that achieves ministry and growth is the primary job of the elder/pastor.

Your elder needs help to do it well. Your elder needs people on the team who are willing to serve and ready to help. Cooperating with your elders while working in submission to them will cause their work to be a joy. The result of working together in the kind of team environment described by Scripture will be nothing short of miraculous.

Build your team! Organize your elders/pastors in such a way as to allow them to be effective at doing the work of administration and oversight (managing), shepherding and pastoring (mentoring), and preaching and teaching (The Word) so the saints can be equipped and deployed for ministry. Do your part to help them accomplish this. I have suggested there is a limit to the number of people any one elder can shepherd effectively. This is why I believe there is a need for more shepherding elders as the church grows.

Every elder has the capacity to manage a limited number of people well. They are to teach, encourage, mentor and guide while working alongside them. The task is for them to duplicate themselves so that disciples learn how to make more disciples. It is imperative for elders to be in relationship with people in order to mentor them. The job becomes overwhelming when there are more people to mentor than one person can manage. This problem burns more elders out over time than any other and becomes a major obstacle to healthy church growth. The solution is for good organization and teamwork among administrative elders, teaching elders, and shepherding elders. A growing church will probably need more shepherding elders than any other kind.

Each shepherding elder can be responsible for mentoring and working with a manageable number of disciples who have a passion for shepherding and care ministry. These maturing disciples in turn can be placed in a leadership position over a ministry team or small group. By focusing on the leaders and deploying them to shepherd the members of their groups, an elder's work can be multiplied quite effectively.

How to Multiply the Ministry of Shepherding Elders

As I bring this book to a close, I would like to help you catch a vision for a team ministry that could multiply the effect of your elders' shepherding and disciple making ministry. A vision describes what you hope to look like in the future as compared to what you look like now. Imagine if you could take a sort of magic telescope that brings the future into focus. When you look at your church through this device, bringing into focus what you would look like if you were achieving ministry the way you think it should be done, you have a vision. If you can write it down and explain it to someone else, you have a vision statement. If you can create a workable process that will take you there, you have a plan.

It seems to me that Scripture provides a compelling picture of servant leadership that teaches and trains, mentors and guides, organizes and manages. When Moses was faced with the impossible task of managing all the people, God provided excellent advice (Deuteronomy 1:9-16). He suggested an organizational model designed to spread the work among the leaders of Israel. Moses proposed the idea to the people, and they agreed it was good, much like the folks who raised their hands in Acts chapter 6. Moses selected leaders to be over groups of ten. Today we might call this a "small group" or "ministry team." He placed leaders over groups of a hundred. We might picture this as an arrangement of ten small groups who report to one leader. He assigned some leaders to be over groups of a thousand. We can imagine the elder board, senior pastor, and staff easily here.

The following diagrams (The Cell, The Molecule and The Body) represent my vision for multiplying the shepherding ministry of the elder: a ministry that plugs more people into the process of being a disciple while helping others become disciples too. At the heart of this multiplication of ministry is the need for elders/pastors and leaders to duplicate themselves. It assumes a desire for people to be committed to doing life together. The team ministry and small group model are very good places to start.

The cell is the smallest unit, representing a small group, a ministry team or members of a care ministry.

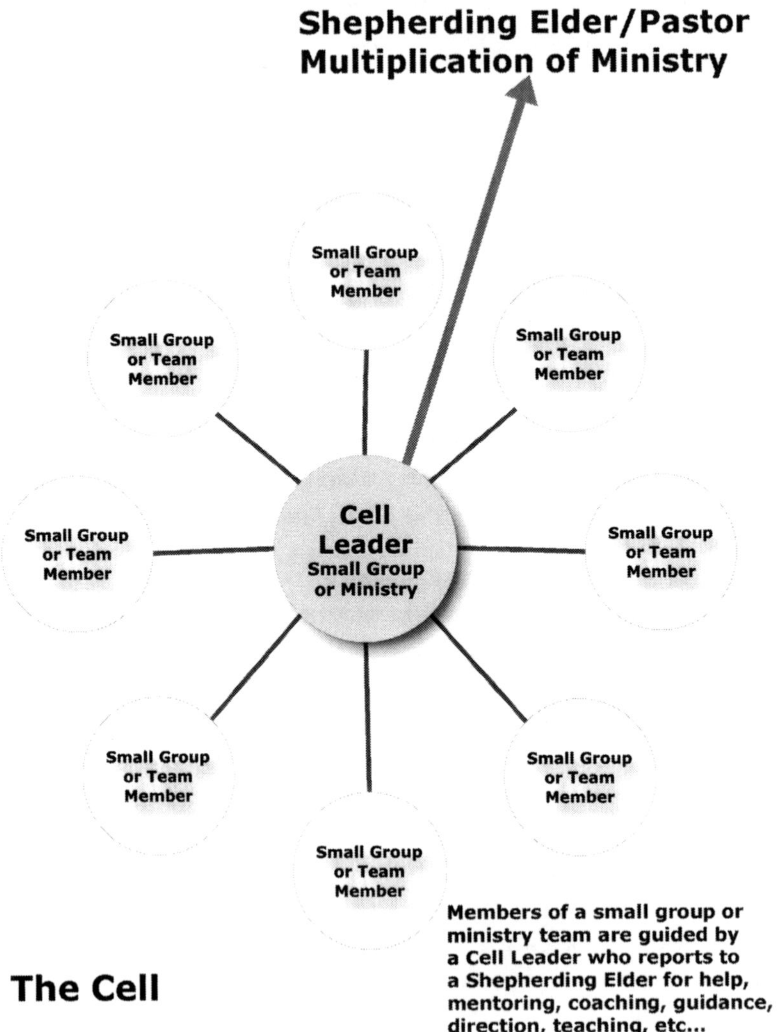

The cell represents a single ministry team or small group. Each cell is assigned a leader, who is guided and coached by a shepherding elder, who spends most of the time working with these leaders. How many cells can an elder manage? While no one knows, each elder has a limit, though the limit differs from elder to elder. When elders reach the limit of their management ability, it is time to add another elder! Over time, it is quite possible that additional shepherds will come from the ministry team or small group cell itself. You may call them "shepherds" or "ministers" or "something else" but the point is, more people are needed who will function like a shepherding elder.

The molecule is a group of cells or cluster of small groups and teams.

Shepherding Elder/Pastor
Multiplication of Ministry

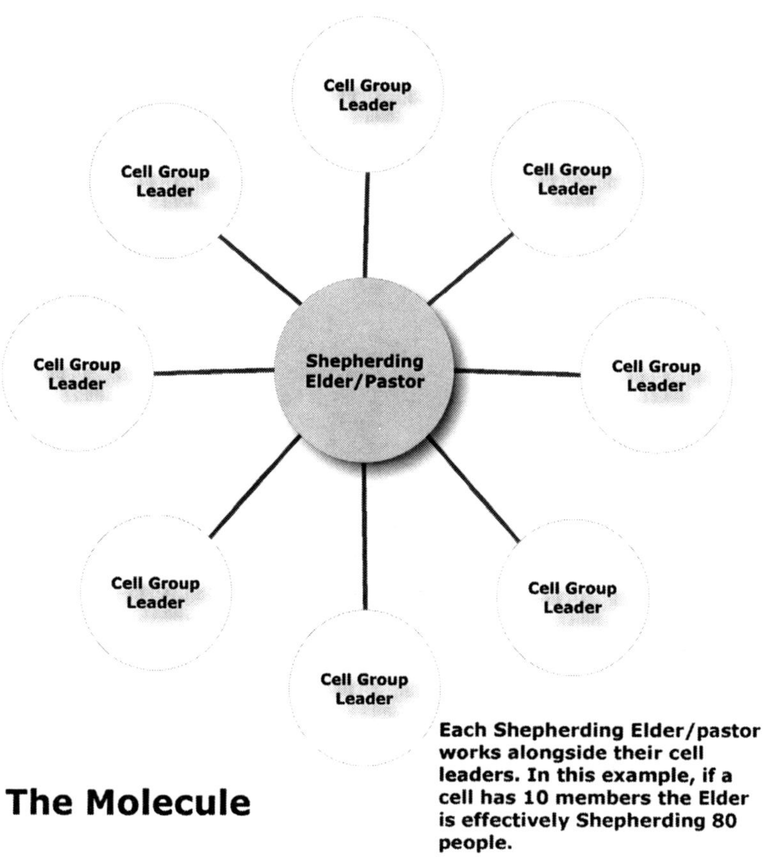

The molecule represents a group of cells, whose leaders are all coached by a shepherding elder. This is similar to a small house church, within the larger church. Here the shepherding elder provides the support and mentoring, the coaching and teaching, and passes on the instructions given by the elder board. This elder coordinates between administrative and teaching elders and cell leaders. The goal is to provide the mentoring needed for spiritual growth and discipleship while keeping everyone on track to achieve the mission. It should be noted that every cell and every molecule will develop a personality of its own. Each one will gravitate toward a ministry of its own. Since each group will have its own unique combination of people and gifts, it is only natural for every group to develop its own passion and ministry. Just keep them focused on the big picture and let the Holy Spirit accomplish it through them in their own unique way. There is much room for diversity and flexibility.

The body is made up of molecules that form the entire church.

Shepherding Elder/Pastor
Multiplication of Ministry

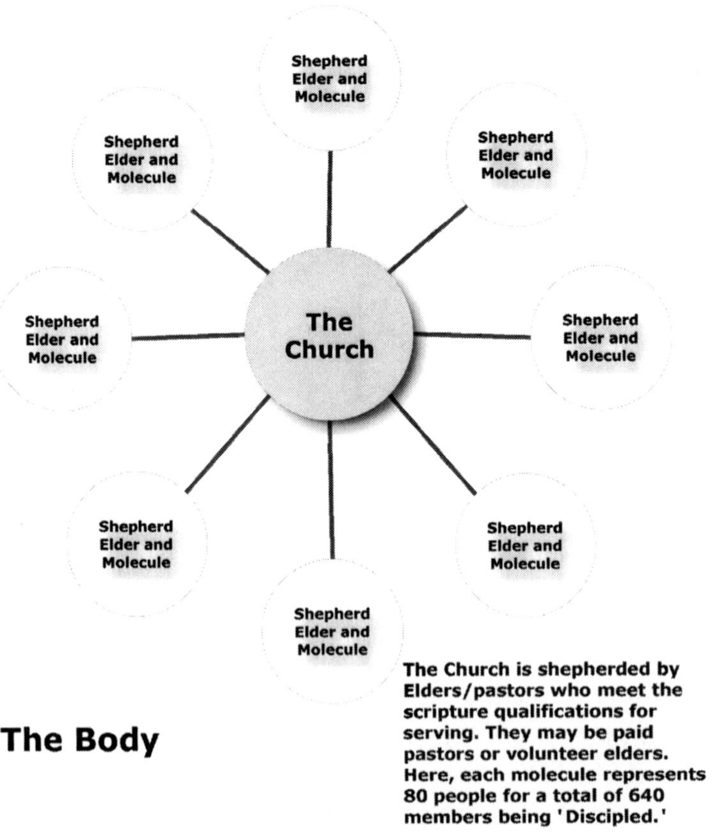

The body represents all of the elders/pastors along with the small group and ministry team leaders and members forming the congregation. In addition, however, many other people will attend church but fail to get plugged in and involved. When we fail to get new believers into mentoring relationships with mature Christians, they are likely to fall away. It is highly unlikely that a new believer will grow in maturity as a disciple without involvement and training. The goal is to encourage new members to become involved. The process of discipleship takes time. It requires commitment to becoming involved with people as we learn and apply God's Word while doing the work of ministry. It becomes difficult when life is so filled with things to do that participation in church is a burden. If we would live as if Heaven were our true home, it would change our priorities.

It seems a reality that most people do not have time for anything beyond church attendance. Could this be caused by a life focused on themselves, the world, and things other than God and being a laborer for Him? What people value most is what they will spend their time doing. I have heard it said that eighty percent of the work in church is being done by twenty percent of the members. What would happen if we could increase the number of people really engaged in ministry to perhaps thirty percent or fifty percent? Can you imagine what would happen in our community, in our country? The truth is, people need to be invited to get involved with ministry. People want to feel needed, and we cannot leave it up to the individual to find their own way into a mentoring relationship, a small group, or ministry. They need constant encouragement by a church community that really values serving each other out of their love for God. When this becomes the priority of our leaders, people will rearrange their schedules and get involved in increasing numbers.

The administrative elders communicate the ministry objectives and keep the church focused on the big picture. The teaching elders teach the Word and oversee the teaching ministry, and the shepherding elders facilitate the mentoring and ministry work. It is okay to call them pastors! It is also okay to call them something else as long as they function as shepherds and mentors. To function well, everyone needs to understand their part and cooperate with each other. It is entirely possible for one elder to function in more than one of these categories and even all three! In a small church, the senior pastor is typically responsible for it all.

In a large church, the senior pastor often works with a board of some kind to head up the administration and oversight and also does the majority of the teaching and preaching. Again, flexibility is allowed. You are free to develop your team according to your needs and the people you have available. You can use job titles and descriptions that fit your circumstances as you are guided by the Holy Spirit. As you catch the vision, it will take shape in your body differently than in others (See Table 7: Balanced Elder/Pastor Team).

Summary and Conclusion: "Hypocrite or Saint?"

The favorite word used by non-believers to describe a Christian is "hypocrite." I like to say, "That's okay; you can join us because we can always use another!" It isn't even a valid argument because they use the term to deflect their own need for a Savior. A Christian is still a person after all and filled with imperfection. It is grossly unfair to expect perfection from a follower of Christ. I love the old saying, "If you find the perfect church, stay away from it because you will ruin it!"

The stinging charge found in the cry, "Hypocrite," is not without merit. We tend to be quite shallow in our attempt to define the difference between us and them. We need to get away from trying to follow some list of do's and don'ts that define our rules for Christianity and focus instead on the condition of our own hearts. We tend to justify ourselves by comparison to others, making ourselves feel better by suggesting that someone else's sin is worse than ours, which makes us okay in some confused manner of thinking. In reality, though, stealing a paper clip is no different in the eyes of Christ than stealing millions. A broken relationship caused by dysfunction among believers is no different than those broken among unbelievers. Sin is sin. Address it.

Many Christians describe themselves as having been liberated from following some list of rules and codes of conduct. To many, importance is placed on becoming free from legalism in order to reach the lost, but often at the cost of caring for the saved. I agree wholeheartedly in doing away with legalism though because legalism and finger pointing create barriers that keep the lost from feeling welcome. Jesus welcomed sinners and so should we. Even so, many who attempt to shed legalism and all things that appear "churchy" continue to miss the point and fail to demonstrate to others the stamp of eternity that Christ made in His own blood for us.

It is essential to demonstrate this stamp of eternity by our love and service to each other as we teach believers how to be disciples. Our relationship with each other should be a visible example to the lost of what it looks like to live together for Christ. If you have stressful and difficult relationships that cause high turnover among your leaders and staff, consider what is going on at the top. Dysfunction among elders, pastors and staff will work its way through your entire church and cause high turnover. Ultimately it is how we model servant relationships at the leadership level that will help mentor the flock toward a more serious walk with Christ. This is why the leaders of a church, those who keep watch over the flock, will be held to account (Hebrews 13:17). And this is why I believe the church in America today has a crisis of leadership.

However, becoming a Christian does not make you perfect; it simply guarantees a safe transition from here to heaven when we die. Consider the alternative and shudder. We need to remember our first love and serve Him with all our heart, and serve our neighbor as ourselves. If we would live our life like this and respond to the love of Christ as His genuine disciples, there would be a real difference in how we do life together, and the world will notice it.[96] A life lived like this has no condemnation. When Jesus taught on loving God and each other, He said, *"All the law and the Prophets hang on these two commandments"* (Matthew 22:40). Against such things there is no law! (Romans 4:15; 5:13, Gal 5:23).

The Christian life is all about responding to the knowledge of where our true home is, and it is not here. We are called to be ambassadors of Christ, which implies being a representative of our heavenly home as we live temporarily here on earth. In Christ, we have been given a choice to become the permanently adopted citizens of heaven while living temporarily as foreigners to earth, or to live temporarily as citizens of earth and permanently as foreigners to heaven. Either we live for ourselves or for God and others. We cannot do both (Matthew 6:24-34). The one will simply be a manipulator of others in order to get what they want (selfish). The other will be in love with God and dedicated to serving His people in order to achieve true joy in living (selfless).

Disciples know where their true home is. Discipleship that leads steadily toward Christian maturity and obedience is at the core of our call to ministry. Accomplishing it requires a structure that works and leaders that people will follow. I submit the Bible has provided the structure, and all we need to do is follow it. God will bring the increase. We are to do our part and trust God to do His. Ministry for Christ is best accomplished when good people commit to working together in loving and obedient relationships, dedicated to a common purpose. Both the purpose and the method of achieving it have been given in God's Word. Since everyone has a unique SHAPE, there is room for flexibility as we put them together to work toward accomplishing our mission. We do not serve a God of "sameness" but of "diversity." Just look at creation and know this truth.

There can be no doubt that Scripture expects certain things of us as we live our lives for Christ. The relationship we have with each other is important. The love and care we have for each other should tell a story without words, a story that allows the Holy Spirit in us to do His work of convincing people of their need for a Savior. The organizational structure found in Scripture is quite compelling. We serve a God of order who has provided clear instructions, but with great flexibility in how to implement it.

The words elder, pastor, shepherd, overseer and bishop are all words that refer to the same person. The elders/pastors are the primary leaders in God's system of government. They are expected to exercise their authority as servant leaders through the teaching and application of God's Word while also caring for their flock. People who become followers of Christ are to obey their leaders as they learn to obey His commands, found in His Word. They need to be trained and equipped for ministry, which the Bible calls "acts of service." Elders are to set the example for the flock to follow while teaching them how to live a full life in Christ. As people take hold of the hand of their elder, the result should be a life that moves toward Christ-likeness. Try asking your staff and leaders how they feel about the work environment created by your elders and pastors. Be honest, be brave and be ready to address areas that may need to change. An elder will be held to a higher level of accountability than anyone else, so take the job seriously and manage well!

Deacons (servants) are the grease that make the machinery of the church run smoothly. These people form a team in support of the work of the elders, freeing them to do their job. While the elder is focused mostly on people, the deacon is focused mostly on "things" that need to be done. A deacon is a mature believer, a disciple of Christ, a student of the Word, and a lover of helping others. Though everyone is called to serve, some are called to occupy that special office called "the office of deacon." However, Scripture does not elevate the Deacon to a higher authority than the elder. The office is a subordinate one in God's Word.

Members include all the saints who have made the decision to trust in Christ alone for their salvation. They are asked to "take up the cross and follow Jesus." Elders are to lead them, while teaching them how to live the life of a believer. As members grow in Christian maturity, they will learn how to make disciples and the church will grow as God adds to its number daily.

The Path to Maturity and Discipleship

My personal mission statement summarizes our responsibility to work toward accomplishing the mission of the church. It can be stated: "All to maturity and many to leadership as we share Christ's love with others." Teamwork is the key to success in ministry because the body of Christ is made up of people working in relationship with each other. This is the essence of "team" and a picture of the "church." Romans chapter 12 offers a wonderful description of the teamwork expected of us. Through teamwork we need a process following Biblical principles. This system will attract people from the community to attend, encourage them to make a decision for Christ, and get them plugged into church life while moving them toward maturity, discipleship, and leadership.

Beware of appearing legalistic because of the barriers it puts up, keeping people from feeling welcome and accepted. Jesus did not have barriers that kept him from loving people who were in sin and neither should we. However, we should be equally careful not to water down the teaching of Scripture, since Christ expects his followers to repent of their sin and change how they live. It is a tightrope to walk, to be sure. A balance should be struck between the love and acceptance of non-believers while helping believers live according to the teaching of Christ. Success at achieving the fivefold purpose means leading people along a path to maturity as we walk the walk we talk.

I described how the process looks like a bicycle where the front wheel represents evangelism and the back wheel discipleship. Does your church look like one of those old fashioned bikes with a huge front wheel and a tiny little back wheel? Perhaps it looks the opposite with a castor on the front and a big wheel on the back. Or maybe you ride one of those unicycles! It is important to fill leadership roles with people who are making progress, without requiring perfection! Leaders should come from among your most mature believers and there should be more balance between the front wheel of evangelism and the back wheel of discipleship.

The following and final chart attempts to picture this process for you. By doing life together in a way that demonstrates our love for God by our love for each other we become noticed by the community. I know of one large church that has such a high rate of burnout and turnover among its leaders and staff that its reputation in the community for having a hard heart is well known. Our service in the community should create an accepting and non-threatening environment that makes people feel welcome because of our love for each other. After they begin attending, we can teach them about their need for a Savior and encourage them toward salvation and membership. After that, we are to show them how they are to live by setting an example for them to follow, an example that obeys Christ and seeks to become more like Him. We don't like the word "obey" very much. But it is the word used in Scripture, and it is part of the mission Christ gave us.

We cannot just leave people at the altar with their hands in the air. We need to show them how to deal with their sin and live life for Christ, and we cannot do so if we are not also addressing the sin and dysfunction in our own lives. We should help them grow in maturity, train them as disciples, and encourage them to be involved with community. Church is far better than any country club could hope to be! All should serve; many will lead. What an awesome life we live as disciples of Christ!

TABLE 14: The Path to Maturity

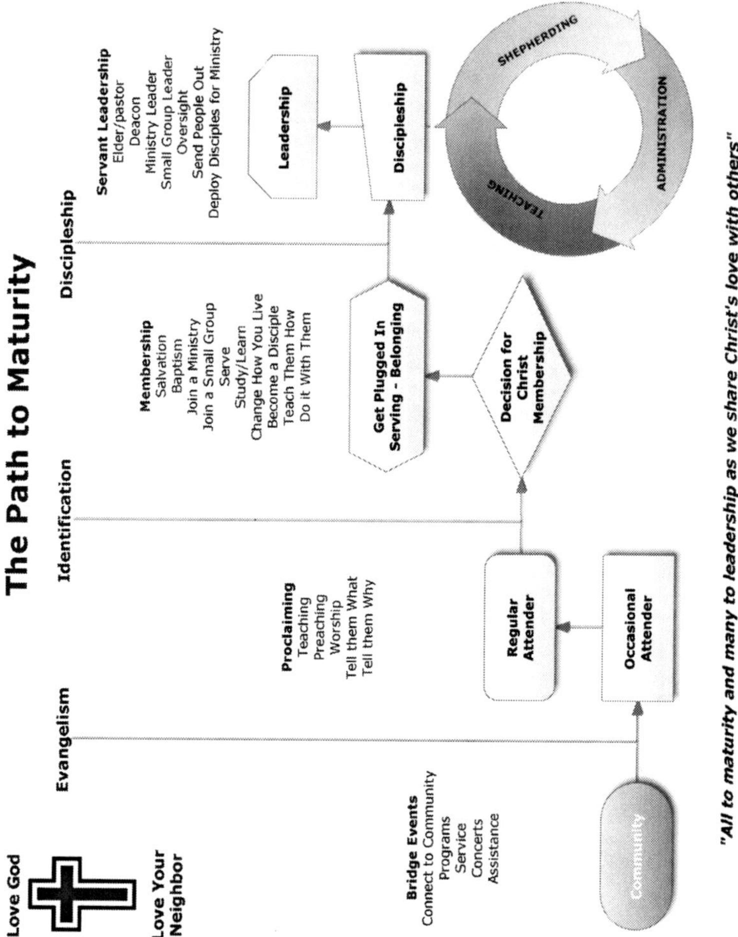

I pray this book has been encouraging to you. I pray especially that it will help you implement a system of government and organization that will allow you to accomplish the mission we have been given. Perhaps it will help you to better understand who an elder is and what an elder does.

Now "GO" - Build your team and make disciples! Demonstrate your love of Christ by your love for each other. The Holy Spirit will help you achieve the mission and God will bring the increase, so trust Him.

THE END

Endnotes

Chapter 1

1. Unless otherwise indicated, Scripture is from the HOLY BIBLE, NEW INTERNATIONAL VERSION®. NIV®. Copyright© 1973, 1978, 1984 by International Bible Society. Used by permission of Zondervan. All rights reserved.

2. J.B. Watson, *The Church: A Symposium of Principles and Practices* (London: Pickering and Inglis, 1949), 82.

3. Mortimer J. Adler, and Charles Van Doren, *How to Read a Book* (New York: Touchstone, 1972), 27.

4. Vines, W.E., Unger, Merrill F., and White, William Jr., *Vines Complete Expository Dictionary of Old and New Testament Words* (Nashville: Thomas Nelson, 1980), 232.

5. Vines, 576.

6. ChangingMinds.Org. December 10, 2010 http://changingminds.org/explanations/needs/maslow.htm

7. About.com Psychology. December 10, 2010. http://psychology.about.com/od/theoriesofpersonality/a/hierarchyneeds.htm

8. Joseph Stowell, *Shepherding the Church: Effective Spiritual Leadership in a Changing Culture* (Chicago: Moody, 1997), 41.

9. Raju D. Kunjummen (Verbal Participle of Attendant Circumstance), *New Testament Greek: A Whole Language Approach* (Troy: Emet, 2009), 361.

10. Kunjummen, 364.

11. Ann Spangler and Lois Tverberg, *Sitting at the Feet of Rabbi Jesus* (Grand Rapids: Zondervan, 2009), 54.

12. Ann Spangler and Lois Tverber, 25.

13. Bible Works for Windows V6.0.012z. Copyright 2003 BibleWorks, LLC *Robertsons Word Pictures* **Mat 11:29 - Take my yoke upon you and learn of me.** The rabbis used yoke for school as many pupils find it now a yoke.

14. Jelinek, John *A Quote delivered during class, "Systematic Theology"* Moody Theological Seminary - Michigan, 2001.

15. David S. Dockery, Kenneth A. Mathews and Robert B. Sloan, *Foundations For Biblical Interpretation: A Complete Library of Tools and Resources* (Nashville: Broadmand & Holman, 1994), 558.

16. David S. Dockery, 560

Chapter 2

17. Rev. Arnold T. Olson, *This We Believe* (Free Church Publications, 1961)

18. Robinson, Hadden W. "Politics and Preaching in the English Reformation." *Bibliotheca Sacra* 122, no. 486 (1965): 121-134.

19. Clowney, Edmund P. "The Politics of The Kingdom." *The Westminster Theological Journal* 41, no.2 (1979): 292-311.

20. Sawatsky, Rev. Ben A. "In Search of a Definition," *The Evangelical Beacon*, 10 August, 1987, 8.

21. Decker, Rodney J. "Polity and the Elder Issue." *Grace Theological Journal* 9, no. 2 (1988): 258-277.

22. Fee, Gordon D. "Reflections on Church Order in the Pastoral Epistles, With Further Reflection on the Hermeneutics of Ad Hoc Documents." *Journal of the Evangelical Theological Society* 28, no. 2 (1985): 141-151.

23. C. Peter Wagner, *Leadership Handbook of Management and Administration: Leading Versus Enabling* (Grand Rapids: Baker, 1994), 152.

24. Hanks, Joyce M. "The Politics of God and The Politics of Ellul." *Journal of Evangelical Theology* 35, no. 2 (1992): 218-278.

25. William Warren Bartley, *Werner Erhard: the transformation of a man: the founding of est.* New York: Clarkson N. Potter, 1978), 118.

26. Engstrom, TedW., Enright, William G., Jones, Ezra E., Robinson, Haddon W. "Leadership Forum: Power, Preaching, and Priorities." *Leadership: A Practical Journal for Church Leaders* 1, no. 1 (1980): 11-28.

27. Mohler, R. Albert, *He is Not Silent: Preaching in a Postmodern World* (Moody:2008), 65.

28. J.B. Watson, *The Church: A Symposium of Principles and Practices* (London:Pickering and Inglis, 1949), 82.

29. J. B. Watson, 91.

30. Mappes, David. "The Laying on of Hands of Elders." *Bibliotheca Sacra* 154, no. 616 (1997): 474-480.

31. Mappes, David. "The Discipline of a Sinning Elder." *Bibliotheca Sacra* 154, no. 615 (1997): 334-343.

32. Chuck Warren, *Variables in Congregationalism: Dynamics in Church Polity – The People and their Leaders* Working Document, EFCA June 1999.

Chapter 3

33. Mark Twain, *The Adventures of Huckleberry Finn* (1884; reprint, Pan Books, 1968), 347.

34. Scott, John R. W., "Christian Ministry in the 21st Century: Part 4 'Ideals of Pastoral Ministry'." *Bibliotheca Sacra* 146, no. 581 (1989): 4-11.

35. John Carnell Edward, *Basic Christian Doctrine: The Government of the Church* (New York: Holt, Rinehart and Winston, 1962), 250.

36. R. Laird Harris, Gleason L. Archer, Jr., and Bruce K. Waltke, *Theological Wordbook of the Old Testament* v1. (Moody: Chicago, 1980), 574.

37. See Appendix "B" *Special Supplement: Elders in the Old Testament*

38. Glassoc, Ed., "The Biblical Concept of Elder," *Bibliotheca Sacra* 144, no. 573 (1987): 67-78.

39. Johnson, John E. "The Old Testament Offices as Pardigm for Pastoral Identity." *Bibliotheca Sacra* 152, no. 606 (1995): 182-200.

40. Gerard Berghoef and Lester De Koster, *The Elders Handbook: A Practical Guide for Church Leaders* (Grand Rapids: Christian Library Press, 1979), 225.

41. David Douglas Bannerman. *The Scripture Doctrine of the Church Historically and Exegetically Considered* (Grand Rapids: Eerdmans, 1955), 416.

42. Howell Jr., Don N. "Confidence in the Spirit as the Governing Ethos of the Pauline Mission." *Trinity Journal* 17, no. 2 (1996): 204-221.

43. Miller, David W. "The Uniqueness of New Testament Eldership." *Grace Theological Journal* 6, no. 2 (1985): 316-329.

44. John Carnell, 252.

45. Osborn, Larry W. "Change Diplomacy." *Leadership: A Practical Journal for Church Leaders* 8, no. 4 (1987): 58-64.

46. Young, Jerry R. "Shepherds, Lead!" *Grace Theological Journal* 6, no. 2 (1985): 329-335.

47. Luter, Boyd Jr. "New Testament Church Government: Fidelity and Flexibility." *Michigan Theological Journal* 2, no. 2 (1991): 127-136.

48. NASB refers to "Scripture taken from the New American Standard Bible®, Copyright © 1960, 1962, 1963, 1968, 1971, 1972, 1973, 1975, 1977, 1995 by The Lockman Foundation. Used by permission."

49. James I. Packer, *Basic Christian Doctrine: The Nature of the Church* (New York: Hold, Rinehart and Winston, 1962), 245.

50. Mappes, David. "The 'Elder' in the Old and New Testaments." *Bibliotheca Sacra* 154, no. 613 (1997): 81-93.

51. Mappes, David. "The New Testament Elder, Overseer, and Pastor." *Bibliotheca Sacra* 154, no. 614 (1997): 163-175.

52. St. John, Matthew R. "Augustine's Self Watch: A Model for Pastoral Leadership." *Bibliotheca Sacra* 155, no. 617 (1998): 93-128.

53. See Appendix B, *Word Studies.*

54. (BDB) F. Brown, C. Driver, and C. Briggs, *Hebrew and English Lexicon* 4th Edition. (Hendrickson: Peabody, 1999), 278.

55. (BAGD) Arndt, William F. and Gingrich, Wilbur F. *A Greek English Lexicon of the New Testament.* 2nd Edition. (Chicago Press: Chicago, 1979), 699.

56. (BROWN) Brown, Colin. *Dictionary of New Testament Theology Vol 1-4. (*Zondervan: Grand Rapids, 1971), I, p. 192.

57. (TDNT) Kittel, Gerhard. (Editor) *Theological Dictionary of the New Testament Vol 1-10.* (Eerdmans: Grand Rapids, 1999), VI. 651.

58. (BAGD), 298.

59. (M&M) Moulton, J.H. and Milligan, G. *Vocabulary of the Greek Testament.* (Hendrickson: Peabody, 1930), 244.

60. (BROWN), I. p.188.

61. (TDNT), II. p.603.

62. Robert C. Anderson, *The Effective Pastor* (Chicago: Moody, 1985), 3.

63. (BAGD), 683.

64. (M&M), 524.

65. (BROWN), Volume 1, 191.

66. (TDNT), Volume VI, 490.

67. Hiebert, Edmond D. "Counsel for Christ's Under-Shepherds: An Exposition of 1 Peter 5:1-4." *Bibliotheca Sacra* 139, no. 556 (1982): 331-342.

68. (BAGD), 342.

69. (BROWN), 929.

70. (TDNT), Volume 1, 907.

71. (BAGD), 559.

72. Berghoef and Koster, 224.

73. Robert C. Anderson, 159.

74. Greg Ogden, *Leadership Handbook of Management and Administration: Servant Leadership* (Grand Rapids: Baker, 1994), 150-151.

75. Litfin, Duane A. "The Nature of the Pastoral Role: The Leader as Completer." *Bibliotheca Sacra* 139, no. 553 (1982): 58-72.

Chapter 4

76. John MacArthur, Church Leadership Series *Qualified Servants for the Church – Deacons (Part 1),* All Rights Reserved: Cassette Tape GC 54-25.

77. Berghoef and Koster, 228.

78. John F. MacArthur Jr., *Ashamed of the Gospel* (Wheaton: Crossway, 1993), 24.

79. Robert C. Anderson, 4.

80. Kent, Homer A. "Obligations of a Pastor and Congregation to Each Other." *Bibliotheca Sacra* 124, no. 496 (1967): 333-349.

81. Ken Blanchard and Phil Hodges, *Lead Like Jesus.* (Nashville: W Publishing, 2005), 26.

82. R. Albert Mohler, Jr. *He is Not Silent: Preaching in a Postmodern World.* (Chicago: Moody, 2008) Mohler, 77.

83. Mohler, 79

Chapter 5

84. Rick Warren, *The Purpose Driven Life.* (Grand Rapids: Zondervan, 2002), 236.

85. Rick Warren, *The Purpose Driven Church.* (Grand Rapids: Zondervan, 1995), 49.

86. Bill Hull, *The Disciple Making Pastor – Leading Others on the Journey of Faith.* (Grand Rapids: Baker, 2007), 97.

87. Joseph Stowell, 41.

88. Bill Hull, 281.

Chapter 6

89. ESV refers to "Scripture quotations from The Holy Bible, English Standard Version® (ESV®), copyright © 2001 by Crossway, a publishing ministry of Good News Publishers. Used by permission. All rights reserved.

90. See Appendix D: Word Studies "Deacon."

91. (M&M), 149.

92. (BROWN), I.p.544-549.

93. (TDNT), V11, p.88-92.

94. Teamwork quotes and proverbs, http://www.heartquotes.net/teamwork-quotes.html, Dec 10, 2010.

95. Tim LaHaye, *Why You Act The Way You Do.* (Illinois: Tyndale, 1984), 25.

Chapter 7

96. Joseph Stowell, *Strength for the Journey.* (Moody: Chicago, 2002), Devotion for December 18/365.

APPENDIX A: WORD STUDIES

1) πρεσβύτερος	Elder/Presbyter
2) ἐπίσκοπος	Overseer/Bishop
3) ποιμήν	Pastor/Shepherd
4) ἡγουμένοις	Leader/Governor
5) οἰκονόμον	Steward/Manager
6) διάκονος	Servant/Minister/Deacon

Resources used in the word study

(*TDNT*) Kittel, Gerhard. (Editor) *Theological Dictionary of the New Testament Vol 1-10.* Eerdmans: Grand Rapids, 1999.

(*BROWN*) Brown, Colin. *Dictionary of New Testament Theology Vol 1-4.* Zondervan: Grand Rapids, 1971.

(*M&M*) Moulton, J.H. and Milligan, G. *Vocabulary of the Greek Testament.* Hendrickson: Peabody, 1930.

(*BAGD*) Arndt, William F. and Gingrich, Wilbur F. *A Greek English Lexicon of the New Testament.* 2nd Edition. Chicago Press: Chicago, 1979.

(*BWW60*) Bible Works for Windows V6.0.012z. Copyright 2003 BibleWorks, LLC.

(*BDB*) F. Brown, C. Driver, and C. Briggs, *Hebrew and English Lexicon* 4th Edition. Hendrickson: Peabody, 1999.

(***TWOT***) Harris, R. Laird, Archer Jr., Gleason L., and Waltke, Bruce K. *Theological Wordbook of the Old Testament* Moody: Chicago, 1980.

(EOBD) Archer Jr., Gleason L., *Encyclopedia of Bible Difficulties* Grand Rapids: Zondervan, 1982.

(VINES) Vine, W.E., Merrill, F., White Jr., William, *Vine's Complete Expository Dictionary of Old and New Testament Words* Nashville: Thomas Nelson, 1984.

Elder/Presbyter πρεσβύτερος ,πρεσβειά πρεσβυτέριον.

(BBW40) The word Occurs 77 times throughout the New Testament, with the greatest concentration found in Acts (25%). The word is found in 16 variants and used in the majority of New Testament books. ***Here it describes a messenger*** (Luke 14:32, Luke 19:14), ***ambassador for Christ*** (2 Cor. 5:20, Eph. 6:20, 2John 1:1), ***older man*** (Titus 2:2; 1Tim. 5:1, Luke 1:18, Phm. 1:9), ***older woman*** (Titus 2:3; 5:2), ***council body of ruling elders*** (Luke 20:10; 22:66, Acts 2:17; 4:8; 4:23; 15:6; 15:22-23; 21:18; 22:5; 23:14; 25:15, 1 Tim. 4:14, Matt. 21:23; 26:3; 26:57; 27:1; 27:3, 27:20, Mark 11:27; 14:53, 1Tim. 5:17, Heb 11:2, Rev. 4:10; 5:8; 5:14; 11:16; 19:4, 1Pet. 5:5), ***an elder as in a member of the ruling body of elders*** (1Tim. 5:15). The word and its variants are widely dispersed throughout the New Testament including the Book of Revelation.

(BAGD): (p. 699) πρεσβεία an ambassador as in "an ambassador for or on behalf of Christ;" πρεσβυτέριον (1.) the highest ruling Jewish council in Jerusalem, (2.) a Christian church council with members expected to be obeyed as an apostle, and synonymous with the term "Bishop" as described below; πρεσβύτερος (2.) designation of an official as implied by the Latin word for 'Senator' as in a member of a ruling board for a congregation, (2.a) members of local councils in individual cities, (2.b) among Christians it refers to the same meaning as Jewish custom had come to expect, as well as to designate civic and religious officials.

(M&M): (p. 534) πρεσβεία "the office of an ambassador;" (p. 535) πρεσβύτερος (1) "in the literal sense an older person;" (3) "an honorific title of office as in village or communal officers."

(BROWN): (I, p.192) be older, be an ambassador, to rule; a council of elders, the rank of elder, be at the head of rule or administration. (1.a.) In the order of society the elders receive respect and authority; (1.d.) referring to the activity of an ambassador who represents the one(s) who have sent him, the plural form appears as title for members of a committee who had judicial and administrative duties; (2.) to be set over as with authority to rule; (3.) an interesting connection is made here to the language of sailors in which the word is used in conjunction with that of the action of a helmsman and has come to be associated with those who steer, lead, guide as one who guides 'the ship of state.'

(TDNT): (VI. p.651) (A.1.) in its most common sense it denotes older as opposed to younger. From the first known usage it denotes the idea of venerability, denoting weight or supreme worth; (A.1.c.) there is a twofold meaning, older and as a title of office. At times the meaning is not easily determined. However, a number of passages, such as Mt. 15:2 and Mk. 7:3,5 clearly represent a normative doctrinal position of a person occupying a place of dignity and authority within a community as with leaders of Christian churches duly appointed and charged to fulfill specific functions. (D. p.662) elders were clearly in existence in the first and earliest Christian church in Jerusalem. There appears a close relationship with the apostles themselves. In Acts. 15; 16:4 they clearly function as a supreme court and normative teaching office for the whole church, in a sense patterned after the Jewish Sanhedrin and not just (but also) of the synagogue council where they act as an authority for the whole church. Clearly as the apostles began to disappear, the elder's role became increasingly important as it grew into an ideal, the growth of the church and the existence of older and tested members who could serve as a presbytery (leaders/rulers).

Other Greek Usage

(TDNT): (VI. p.651) (A.1.) Plato emphasized the importance of following advice/council from those who are aged (older and wiser). (A.1.b.) The constitution of Sparta uses the term to denote a political title as in the president of a college; in Egypt (Ptolemaic and Imperial period) is also used as a title, denoting authority as with those in charge of a corporation. It also appears in village government as those who were given authority to rule.

Septuagint and Old Testament Usage

(TDNT): (VI. p.655) (B.) In all strata of the OT tradition the elders are presupposed. Nowhere do we read of their appointment or of the establishment of their colleges. Their origin lies in the most ancient patriarchal period during a time when Israel was made up of tribes, who followed the authority of their tribal leaders. At all times they are representatives of the whole people under leading figures such as Moses and Joshua. When Moses appointed the 70 of Nu. 11:16 we find a transfer of authority and it is at this time that elders began to possess and exercise the authority of an office.

Conclusion

> It seems that πρεσβύτερος (elders) have been in existence from earliest times. Throughout the Old Testament and continuing into the New Testament, elders have occupied an office of authority and rule. Elders are in a position of authority, acting as ambassadors for Christ on behalf of the body of Christ with responsibility to guide the church, as one would steer a "ship of state." The term seems to refer more to the authority of an office such as "an office of government." Therefore, the word conveys a meaning consistent with the idea of an "office of authority" with the expectation that people under them will follow and obey.

Overseer/Bishop ἐπίσκοπος η (ἐπίσκοπεω ἐπίσκοπτομαι)

(BBW40) The word occurs 11 times and pretty evenly distributed across 7 New Testament books. ***Here it describes an office as in an 'office of Bishop'*** (Acts 1:20; 1Tim. 3:1;), ***a visitation from God*** (Luke 19:44, 1Pet. 2:12), ***an overseer, guardian or Bishop*** (Acts 20:28; 1Tim. 3:2; Tit. 1:7; 1Pet. 2:25; Phil. 1:1), and as a verbal participle in the masculine nominative 2nd person plural ἐπισκοποῦντες meaning ***to see after, to oversee, to see to it or take care of***(Heb 12:15; 1Pet. 5:2). The term appears to be synonymous or interchangeable with the previous word, πρεσβύτερος as evidenced by Acts 20:17-28 where Paul calls the πρεσβύτερος (Elders) to meet him and actually refers to them as ἐπίσκοπος (Bishops or Overseers). He then tells them to act like ποιμήν (Pastors or Shepherds) discussed below.

(BAGD): (p.298) ἐπισκοπέω to look at, see to, take care of or oversee. In a distinctly Christian sense it refers to the activity of church officials, particularly those acting as Bishop or Overseer. Also, indication that a person in this position has only God as his personal overseer. (p.299) ἐπισκοπή (1.) a visitation of demonstrations of divine power mostly in the good sense and also a personal visitation of God himself. (p.299) ἐπισκοπος From pre-Christian times it meant overseer, (1.) of God and of Christ, with the meaning expanded to include (2.) of persons who have a definite function or a fixed office within a group, including a religious group. The early church certainly had church officials who occupied this office of Overseer or Bishop.

(M&M): (p.244) ἐπισκοπέω (1983) to exercise oversight or care. ἐπίσκοπος (1985) The use of this word as an official title in pre-Christian times has been fully illustrated by Deissmann. The Christian era from earliest times uses the word to describe the function of one who occupies an office, namely to have the duty for oversight and to act as judge.

(BROWN): (I. p.188) the terms ἐπίσκοπος and πρεσβύτερος are linked by evidence to refer to the same office of function in the early Christian church. Has the general meaning of looking at or paying attention to a person or thing. The verb forms can mean to observe, review, or superintend and also to inspect or examine. (e. p.192) referring to 'office of Bishop' and first used in 1Tim. 3:1 to designate a defined office to which one could aspire. Later, as the Church grew and evolved, attention shifts from the duties (which were already understood at the time) to the personal qualities that are needed for it; personal discipline, a well-ordered family, gifts of teaching and etc. There is no formula for how many men should serve in the office and the number varies. (d.) The development of this position marks a transition from the missionary era of the Church with its charismatic gifts to an institution with permanent character. As the apostles died off, this office provided continuity through which the Church could be properly lead and directed.

(TDNT): (II. p.603) (B.) ἐπίσκοπεω ἐπίσκοπτομαι In the NT, Jesus himself demonstrated a high estimation of the visiting of the sick in Rabbinic ethics. Man has to realize that he does not exist of and for himself but of and for the other. This is to be expressed in his actions. God himself is present in this existence with and for others. In its deepest sense it means to be concerned about others with a sense of responsibility for them. The present stem of the word appears twice in the New Testament and has the sense as found in the LXX of work done by the good shepherd out of concern for his flock. ἐπίσκοπος (A. 2. p.610) denotes the meaning of protective care as the heart of the activity of men so engaged in this office. To oversee is in the same sense as the 'master of a house,' 'a ships captain,' or 'a merchant in charge of various goods.' (A. 4.) It describes those who are the holders of a particular office and described various official actions. The plural form ἐπίσκοποι refers to local officials or officers. It is felt that the Christian usage of the term has its roots in this derivation. It undoubtedly refers to the work of supervision or control, however there is no precision in describing the term. (C. 1.) In 1 Pt.

2:25 Christ Himself is called ἐπίσκοπος and the word seems to strengthen the term ποιμήν described below. In fact, the two words seem to become interchangeable as a description of the duty to keeping watch over the flock. (C. 2.) It refers to the leaders of the Church. (a) The title only appears where there are settled local congregations in which regular acts are performed. (b) From the very first the word had the basic understanding of a holder of an office. (c) The pastorals carry the idea further to describe it as an office that one may seek to hold, and to obtain it there were certain qualifications that must be met. It seems that one of the purposes, if not the main purpose of the office, is to ensure the continued life of the churches once the missionaries had gone.

Other Greek Usage

(TDNT): (II. p.599) In classical Greek the word is derived from the root skop denoting continuous or careful scrutiny. Outside the New Testament ἐπίσκοπεω ἐπίσκοπτομαι (1.a.) follows the sense of 'to look upon, to consider, to have regard for something or someone.' It is used to describe the activity of ancient deities, such as Bachus, who 'graciously look down upon, care for, watch over..' (1.b.) To reflect on something, to examine it, to submit it to investigation. ἐπίσκοπη appears only once in Classical Greek and has the meaning 'to visit.' In non Biblical Greek, ἐπίσκοπος (A.) is best rendered as 'overseer' or 'watch.' In the Christian sense, it develops fuller meaning as 'onlooker,' 'watcher,' 'protector,' 'patron.' With time, the word comes to be used (b.) as a title to denote various offices.

(M&M): (p.244) ἐπίσκοπος (1985) are listed amongst the officials of the temple of Apollo at Rhodes in *ib.*731 and in a curious religious letter referring to them as 'guardians.'

(BROWN): (I. p.188) (3) from Homer onwards it meant 'overseer' and first applied to a deity as one who keeps watch over a country or people. However, the title was also given to men who had a responsible position of state and later this included religious communities. Syrian records use the title for members of a committee of control for building or a board of trustees with decision-making authority.

Septuagint and Old Testament Usage

(TDNT): (II. p.599) (2) In the LXX ἐπίσκοπεω ἐπίσκοπτομαι took on a profound religious meaning within the sense of 'to look upon, to investigate, and in a deeper sense to be concerned about something.' It means to take oversight and in 43 OT passages (Mostly Numbers) it has the meaning 'to muster.' (B. 2.) It also has the meaning of work being done on behalf of a flock by a good shepherd who is concerned most with the welfare of the flock. (B. 3.) It has the meaning 'to appoint someone to an office.' (4. g. p.606) ἐπίσκοπή takes on, in the theological sense, the meaning of 'visitation.' (B. 1. p.614) The general sense of ἐπίσκοπος is of supervisors in various fields.

Conclusion

> Clearly the vast majority of the use of the word *ἐπίσκοπος η οι* is in connection with the holder of an office of some authority. The term, translated as bishop or overseer, becomes synonymous with elder or presbyter and pastor or shepherd. One can aspire to the position, and a worthy aspiration it is. The purpose of the office is to see that the organized church has continuity after the missionary's job is done and an organized body of believers has been formed. The elders also ensure that the body of believers are served, guarded, and shepherded and lead the church in the fulfillment of "The Great Commission." The holder of this position must have specific character qualifications. The duties of the person are to manage, oversee, watch, care for, supervise, lead, teach, preach and rule. In short, the position is one of servant leadership, and it is only logical to conclude that the flock is therefore expected to follow. In this word we gain understanding about "who" should occupy the "office."

Pastor/Shepherd ποιμήν

(BBW40) The word occurs in several derivations 39 times in 11 New Testament books. The majority of these, 45% occur in the 4 gospels. ***Here it serves as a present active infinitive referring to Christ meaning 'who rules'*** (Mat 2:6; Rev 12:5; Rev 2:27; Rev 19:15), ***and also as a future active indicative verb referring to 'shepherd who will lead'*** (Rev 7:17), ***and to 'tend like a shepherd'*** (1Co 9:7; 1Pe 5:2; Joh 21:16; Act 20:28; Luk 17:17), ***as a verbal participle and referring to people who care not about others but rather 'shepherd themselves only'*** (Jud 1:12), ***and as an accusative masculine plural noun meaning 'pastors'*** (Eph 4:11), ***and appearing as an accusative or nominative masculine singular noun referring, either directly or indirectly, to Christ 'The Good Shepherd'*** (Mat 9:36,25:32,

26:31; Mar 6:34, 14:27; Joh 10:2, 10:11, 10:12, 10:14, 16; Heb 13:20; 1Pe 2:25), ***as simple 'shepherds actually tending sheep'*** (Luk 2:8, 2:15, 2:18, 2:20), ***and simply as a 'flock' as in a flock of sheep*** (Luk 2:8, 12:32). It is noteworthy that all instances of the masculine singular noun form of the word are used to refer to 'The Good Shepherd' who is Christ Himself. ***Out of the 39 occurrences, 6 of them refer directly or indirectly to pastors/shepherds/leaders*** (1Co 9:7; 1Pe 5:2; Eph 4:11; Joh 21:16; Act 20:28; Eph 4:11). ***Further, 2 of these include specific instructions for a shepherd to act like ἐπίσκοπος 'overseers'*** (Act 20:28; 1Pe 5:2).

(BAGD): (p.683) ποιμαίνω in the literal sense refers to a shepherd or tending sheep like a shepherd. (2.) When used figuratively it is referring to the activity that protects, guards, rules, governs and (2.a.) in the sense of lead, guide and rule. It is within this figurative sense that the term is used to describe the act of directing a congregation as found in 1Pt 5:2. (2.b.) The meaning includes the sense of protect, care for and nurture. Within the church setting the expectation is for 'shepherds' to lead the congregation. When the word is used to refer to a flock it is, in the literal sense, referring to a flock of sheep. When applied in the figurative sense to the church it is referring to the body of believers with Christ as the head of the church.

(M&M): (p.524) (4165 and 4166) To 'shepherd' and to 'tend' as one would care for a flock. From the idea of pasturing and feeding the verb readily passes into the idea of 'governing' and 'guiding.' Shepherd is a common word and does not always occur in a very favorable light when used in the literal sense.

(BROWN): (I. p.191) (3.a.) The term is used as a title for the exalted Christ and linked to ἐπίσκοπος describing Him as the guardian or overseer of our souls. As a title, it sums up everything the term had come to mean in the OT. It is no accident but the expression of a conscious insight that shepherd is linked with overseer. (II. 412) The essential point regarding a shepherd is in the flocks need for protection and leadership. Without a shepherd to guide them the flock will become scattered because each one will go his own way. (III. p.564) The word is frequently used in a metaphorical sense as leader, ruler, commander. (p.568) (4.) Christian elders were exhorted not to be self-seeking masters over the community, but examples of service to it. The term is used as a description of the duties expected of those who hold the office of overseer, [namely elders]. This function can be deduced from 1Pe 5:2 and Act 20:28 to be that of caring for the spiritual welfare of the flock. In these cases, leaders must prove themselves worthy examples of the flock. Therefore, character attributes become the most important qualities of a person called to act as shepherd.

(TDNT): (VI. p.490) The New Testament has a distinctly positive view of Shepherds. Jesus does not hesitate to use the term as a description of God. (V.) Only once in the New Testament are congregational leaders called shepherds (Eph 4:11). The absence of the article before the word shows that pastors and teachers (shepherds) form a single group, obviously because they minister to the individual congregation. As the church grew and developed, there is always a sense of the metaphor when congregational leaders are called shepherds. In connection with the congregation, these shepherds are the leaders of the local church (also called Bishops). The responsibility is to care for the congregation, to seek the lost, to combat heresy and to be an example for the flock. His work will be recognized by Christ, The Good Shepherd.

Other Greek Usage

(TDNT): (VI. p.486) (B. I.) On a Sumerian royal inscription the king is referred to as a shepherd having been appointed by deity. In Babylonian and Assyrian the term is a common one used to describe a ruler and is a common figure of speech meaning, 'to rule.'

(BROWN): (III. p.564) The word is frequently used in a metaphorical sense as leader, ruler, commander. Plato reminds us of the religious use of the word when he compares the rulers of the city-state to shepherds who care for their flock. In the ancient East the term signified a position of honor and was applied to both divinity and rulers alike.

Septuagint and Old Testament Usage

(TDNT): (VI. p.486) (B. II.) The OT describes Yahweh as the Shepherd of Israel. A great number of OT passages picture God as a Shepherd of the people. However, the term is also used (as in the threats of Jeremiah) to denote political and military leaders. There is a period of time in later Judaism when we find references to shepherds being listed among the thieving and cheating occupations. But by the time of the New Testament it is used in a positive way to describe Christ as The Shepherd. Further, it was understood from early times to be a term used as a comparison to a leader in a community. OT examples of faithful shepherds include Moses and David. Later, the term was commandeered by Christians, which led to a conscious avoidance of using the term by any of the rabbinic writers of the same era.

(BAGD): (p.684) In the LXX it refers to a shepherd or sheepherder. Further, flock (ποίμνιον) is often used to refer to the Jewish people themselves as in Jer 13:17.

(BROWN) (III. p.566) After the exile the Pharisaic rabbis brought about a striking devaluation of the occupation of shepherd in Palestinian Judaism. In a time of poor pay, shepherds were often suspected of dishonesty. This negative view did not carry over into the NT. On the contrary, the shepherd's devotion to duty is painted in glowing colors.

Conclusion

The term pastor or shepherd is associated and practically interchangeable with the words for bishop/overseer and elder/presbyter. The Apostle Paul sent for the elders of the church, and, when speaking to them, he called them bishops/overseers and instructed them to act like shepherds/pastors (Acts 20:17-28). Peter identifies himself as a fellow elder and instructs elders to shepherd the flock while exercising oversight authority over the flock, not as one who lords the position over them but as a servant who loves and leads (1Pet 5:1). The shepherd cares for his congregation, providing leadership, protection, instruction, guidance, oversight, and rule. He occupies an office and should receive honor. He should place the needs of his flock above his own and should never take on the duties of shepherd for personal gain. In this sense, a shepherd must have the character attributes that make him worthy of the calling. He is a servant of Christ who is to set an example for the congregation in order to lead them in "The Way" of Christ while equipping them to serve in ministry for Christ. Finally, in this word we have an action verb (shepherd) describing "what" the person does as he achieves the duties of the office of elder as an overseer. An elder "shepherds" the flock with the authority of an overseer under Christ.

Leader/Ruler/Governor ἡγεμόνα ας ον οων [ἡγουμένον ος οις]

(BBW40) There are 24 occurrences of the word in the New Testament (as a noun or functioning as a noun) in Matthew, Mark, Luke plus Acts and Hebrews. The majority of the instances are in the synoptic gospels. ***In each instance here it means 'governor' or 'ruler'*** (Mat 2:6; 10:18; 27:2; 27:11; 27:14; 27:27; 28:14, Luk 2:2; 3:1; 20:20; 21:12; 22:26, Act 14:12; 23:24; 23:26; 23:33; 24:1, Act 24:10, Mar 13:9). Appearing as a verbal participle (functioning as a noun) [ἡγουμένοις ἡγούμενον] ***has the meaning 'leaders' or more literally 'those who have rule over'*** (Heb 13:17 and Act 7:10), ***and simply as 'leaders'*** (Act 15:22, Heb 13:24). It is quite interesting to note the use of the term in Acts 14:12 where his audience believed Paul to be the holder of a high office, 'chief speaker' and is therefore taken to be Hermes.

(BAGD): (p. 342) ἡγεμόνευω to be leader, command, rule, order of the administration as in a governor; ἡγεμόνια to be chief, command, direction, management of any high office. (1.) of the imperial government and (2.) of the office of governor; ἡγεμόνικος the guiding or leading spirit; ἡγέομαι (1.) lead, guide of men in any leading position, ruler, leader of princely authority, high officials, and military commanders; (2.) to think, regard or consider as in giving consideration or thinking about someone or something.

(M&M): (p. 276) (2230) is applied to the rule of a prefect, (2231) used to describe the office or rule of a prefect, (2232) applied to the position of governor or an officer in general as in a prefect and (2233) certainly denotes a 'superior.'

(BROWN): (p.929) The rules formulated to govern behavior patterns within the Christian household are limited to specific classes as: wives, husbands, children, parents, slaves, masters. Christians are addressed according to their station in life, and especially within the Christian household. The key thought of the New Testament examples is 'submission' and the primary motivation behind these admonitions is that such an attitude expresses subordination to Christ's Lordship. Other blocks of similar material contain encouragements addressed to Christians who are called to be submissive to their church leaders ('overseers', 'elders', deacons') based on earlier teaching in 1Th 5:12, 13; Heb 13:17 where the 'leaders' are commended as worthy of respect and obedience. This is counted as 'virtue' among Christians.

(TDNT): (p.907) (1.) Has the possible meanings of 'to lead', 'to think', 'to believe', to 'regard as.' (2.a.) The plural form is used mostly for leaders of the church community. The community is obviously divided into two groups, those who lead and those who are led. In Heb 13:17 these leaders are pastors responsible to God who has entrusted the other members of the community to them. Those being led owe obedience to those who lead. The founders of the community, who have died are also listed among the leaders and serve as examples of faith. Reverent subjection to human officers with the divinely given pastoral authority is now integral to Christian piety. A suggestion is made in 1 Clement 1,3 that these leaders are distinguished from the elders, which may be a clue about the transition to early Catholicism.

Other Greek Usage

(TDNT): (p.907) (2.b.) The word is widely understood of non-Christian leaders, great men, officials and princes.

Septuagint and Old Testament Usage

(TDNT): (p.907) (2.b.) It is used in the LXX to describe military leaders and leaders of the people.

Conclusion

> Certain people within the Christian community are called to a position of authority and asked to lead the members of the community. This word was clearly understood by original readers to mean "leader or ruler." Specifically, in the church these leaders (elders/overseers/shepherds) are holders of an office, as in an office of government. They are responsible primarily to God and will be held accountable by Him for their actions. They are expected to fulfill the duties of leading the congregation while equipping them for ministry as they exercise oversight authority. Just as a military captain expects obedience from his subordinates, members of the congregation are expected to obey their leaders. A system of government is certainly the expectation in Scripture. Submission (without grumbling but with joy) to the authority of those who occupy leadership positions is a part of Christian piety and a demonstration of obedience to Christ. The key to effectiveness is not found in "lording the position over the people" but in leading by example, as a servant who shows rather than tells, who teaches rather than admonishes.

Steward/Manager οἰκονόμον

(BBW40) The word occurs 20 times in 18 passages and evenly spread through a high percentage of New Testament books. ***Here it means 'manager'*** (Luk 12:42; 16:1-8, Gal 4:2, 1Co 4:2), ***'position of manager'*** (Luk 16:1,3,8, 1Co 9:17, Eph 3:2; Col 1:25; 1Pe 4:10; Tit 1:7, Tit 1:4), ***'administration of' [as in administration of the plan of God]*** (Eph 1:10; 3:9; 1Co 4:1), ***'manager in charge of a city's treasury'*** (Rom 16:23). ***Of particular importance to this study is the impact of Tit 1:7 in which an 'overseer/bishop' is referred to as 'the steward-manager of God.'*** This creates a clear connection between the specific office and its function as one of a manager with responsibility on behalf of God.

(BAGD): (p.559) To be the holder of an office as manager. To manage, regulate, administer, plan. (1.) To provide management of a household, of direction, of an office. (1.a.) It is not always possible to draw a distinction between the office itself and the activities associated with it. (1.b.) Paul clearly applies the idea of administration to the office of apostle and also of the Bishop. (p.560 1.a.) Of the manager in a private position who manages his masters property and is accountable to the owner. (2.) In Tit 1:7 the Bishop is described as God's manager.

(M&M): (p. 442) (3622) Describes the office of οἰκονόμος and suggests that one should take care that persons of repute are appointed to such offices. (3623) In the literal sense it means to be a steward, manager of an estate.

(BROWN): (II. p.253) Management, office, steward, manage, administer and plan.

(I. p697) In Eph 3:1-8 regarding the realization of God's saving plan in Christ, God's house is under discussion. The plan of God serves to characterize God's activity in Christ as the fulfillment of an eternal purpose. It is one in which men do not have a say (that is, men have no say in God's plans). (I. p.738) In Eph 1:10 Paul links – [the administration of God's plan for the house of God] with the fullness of times. He wishes here to stress that the Christ event does not lie in the realm of human factors and possibilities but in the counsel of God (v.9). (p. 254) Something like a specific New Testament usage has been established which has two main different aspects: (1.)(a.) The words are used to denote the occupation of household and estate managers and their tasks. (b.) The position is similar in the rest of the NT. It used by Paul metaphorically to describe the apostolic task. Faithfulness is named as an essential requirement of a steward. In the same way, Tit 1:7 requires that "a bishop, as God's steward, must be blameless." In 1 Pet 4:10 all the members of the (Christian) community are called to be "stewards of God's varied grace." (c.) To understand the concepts of the words one must refer to their roots in the concept of house, as it is in the New Testament οἰκος. God's people, God's community, is his house which he builds up through the work of those he has called to the task, to whom he entrusts the stewardship of the house. They are not to look upon these household affairs as their own; they are merely stewards of the gifts entrusted to them and have to give an account of their stewardship. Paul refers to the preaching of the gospel as a 'commission' from which he cannot withdraw. In Col 1:25 and Eph 3:2 the divine office committed to the apostle is under discussion. (2.) The use of the word moves in a second direction in the sense of God's plan of salvation. But, these two senses are connected because God's plan of salvation is to be proclaimed through men. Therefore, the work of the οἰκονόμος is rooted in the divine οἰκονόμια.

(TDNT): (V. p.119) In the NT, especially the Gospels, the root word is used to describe the house of God, both on earth and in heaven. (6.) The term is used to refer to the 'house of God' in Heb 3:1-6 where it is pointed out that Moses was a servant in the whole house of God while Christ has been set over the house of God. In the NT, οἰκια became associated first with house, and then with 'household' and 'family.' It can also mean 'possession.' (V. p.149) In Greek, the word οἰκονόμος is first used to describe a steward or manager of a house. It is first used in the parables of Jesus. In Mat 24:45 there appears an interchangeability of οἰκονόμος and δοῦλος which shows plainly an identification of someone who is selected from among the servants of a household and placed in a position of stewardship and sometimes over the whole property of his master. Paul uses the word as a figure for apostolic authority and knowledge. Social position is not a consideration at all in the use of this word. The steward in the New Testament Christian is entrusted with the treasures of the Gospel, having knowledge of God's plan of salvation. It is in the use of the word οἰκονόμια that we find 'the office of household administration and the discharge of this office.' Paul frequently uses the word to mean 'plan of salvation,' 'administration of salvation,' and 'order of salvation.'

Other Greek Usage

(TDNT): (V. p.119) The stem οἰκος means house or dwelling and its use as a noun was common in Greek at the time of Homer. Sometimes specific houses are meant and it was used to refer to a 'temple' as well.

(BROWN): (II. p.253) οἰκονόμοια Attested from Xen. and Plato on, denoted primarily the management of a household, but was soon extended to the administration of the state and finally for every kind of activity which results from the holding of an office. οἰκονόμος was used of people and had more concrete meaning. It denotes the house steward and then by extension the managers of individual departments within the household, e.g. the porter, the estate manager, the head cook, the accountant, all domestic officials who were mostly recruited from among the slaves. Similarly οἰκονόμεω means to manage as a house steward, order, regulate.

Septuagint and Old Testament Usage

(TDNT): (V. p120) In the LXX οἰκος is a favorite word. It can denote family, race and is used as a fixed term for the 'sanctuary.' And, it was used to refer to the house of his congregation meaning, 'house of God.'

(BROWN): (II. p.254) The occurance of the words in the LXX does not give much help toward understanding the New Testament concept. οἰκονόμια only occurs in Isa 22:19, 21 and then in the original meaning of adminstration, office. οἰκονόμος appears more frequently and is likewise used in the technical sense of the word for a court official, chiefly the royal palace governor.

Conclusion

A steward is a manager of the affairs and possessions that belong to someone else. In the New Testament, steward comes to rest on the idea of having responsibility to manage the affairs of God on behalf of His household and to share the Gospel message. With stewardship comes the responsibility of management. When the word is linked with overseer (most notably in Tit 1:7) or pastor or shepherd, it simply provides further understanding of the expectation God has for a person occupying the position within His organizational plan. Most people have stewardship responsibility over something (their money, home, business, etc), but an elder has stewardship responsibility over the New Testament Church.

SUPPLEMENTAL WORD STUDY: Elders in the Old Testament

(BBW40) זִקְנֵי zaqen (pronounced Zaw-Kane) appears in the Old Testament 62 times in this form. The word is found in the OT 206 times in various forms. It is translated as 'elder' or 'elders' and here ***it has the meaning of***

'a leader' or 'one who is recognized as being a leader or manager' (Gen 50:7, Exo 3:16; 4:29; 12:21; Num 11:16; 16:25; 22:4. Deu 19:12; 21:20, Jos 20:4, Jdg 11:5; 21:16, Rth 4:4, 1Sa 4:3; 8:4; 15:30, 1Kgs 8:1; 20:7). The scriptures listed are representative of the 62 occurrences in which the meaning is that of a leader with authority. There are many others.

(BDB): (p.278) The word in this specific form has the meaning of 'one who has authority.' It appears in various forms also to mean old, old man, old woman, old human beings, and etc. However, this word most definitely includes a respected position of authority. A leader is implied as in a tribal leader of the people, or a designated leader for the people, or a selected leader or manager of a household as in one of "Pharaohs" house managers.

(TWOT): (v.1, p.574) Meaning aged, ancient, elder, senator. The LXX renders this word as presbuteros and, used adjectively to describe a person (male or female) contrasting them with the youth, meaning old or older from the original meaning of 'beard.' The old or older man is to be honored and respected. The old speak first and are expected to be heard. They are valued as advisors. There is no clearly defined age to qualify as old. Only context can provide clues about the meaning as old man or ruling elder or body. There are elders within a house, such as in Pharaoh's house. The ruling body of the Hebrew city as well as of people like the Moabites and Midianites and Gibeonites were the elders. The elder had become an 'institution' known to the Hittites and the Babylonians from the period of Hammurabi forward. Elders and commanders are frequently combined to form a governing body. Elders who sit at the gate (Deut 21:19; 22:15, Prov 31:23) preside over and settle disputes, ratify property transactions, and try murder cases.

Conclusion

Elders have occupied a position of authority among the people of God from the earliest Biblical times. It is first used by Moses in Numbers 11:16 to create a specific "office" in which an elder is responsible to exercise authority for the people of God. They served as leaders, rulers, and judges and occupied a governing position among the people.

Deacon – Servant - Minister διάκονος ει οις έω

(BBW40) ***Occurrences in NT:*** Occurs nearly 100 times in 17 New Testament Books. The highest concentration of the word is found in letters written by Paul. The word appears in 23 variants having a variety of meaning, depending upon context. ***Here it has the meaning: To serve as in serving others; caring and ministering to people*** (Mat 27:55; Acts 19:22; Rom 12:7; 1Co 16:15; 2Co 3:3; Eph 4:12, 6:21; 2 Tim 4:11; Philemon 1:13; Heb 6:10; 1Pe 4:10, 4:11; Rev 2:19); ***to send or contribute financial support in relief of brothers or a ministry in need of help*** (2Co 8:4, Acts 11:29); ***referring to Elders commitment to work at the ministry of teaching the word of God*** (Acts 6:4); ***the service of ministering Angels sent by God to help those who are being saved*** (Heb 1:14); ***the servant type of leadership expected of Elders who would have oversight authority in the household of God*** (Mat 20:26, 20:28, 22:16, 23:11; Mark 9:35, 10:43, 10:45; Luke 22:26, 22:27); ***a person who serves, helps, obeys and carries out the wishes of the one he serves; who has authority over them like a master or King over a slave; employer over an employee; or as Christ over His servant*** (Matt 22:13; Luke 17:8; John 12:26; Romans 13:4; 2Co 3:6, 6:4, 11:15, 11:23; 1Ti 1:12); ***a good or faithful minister*** (Col 1:7; 1Ti 4:6); ***to fulfill a stated purpose, objective or mission known as a ministry or ministry of service which includes management responsibility*** (Acts 1:17, 1:25, 12:25, 20:24, 21:19; Rom 11:13, 15:8, 15:25, 15:31; 1Co 3:5, 12:5; 2Co 3:7, 3:8, 3:9. 4:1, 5:18, 6:3, 8:19, 8:20, 9:1, 9:12, 9:13, 11:8; Gal 2:17; Eph 3:7; Col 1:23, 1:25, 4:17; 2Ti 4:5); ***a server as in a waiter or waitress*** (Luke 10:40, 12:37; John 2:5, 2:9; Acts 6:1, 6:2); ***to serve as a government official with authority to punish and reward*** (Romans 13:4); ***to serve as a deacon as in the office of Deacon*** (Rom 16:1; Phil 1:1; 1Ti 3:8, 3:10, 3:12, 3:13). The term has a wide range of meaning depending on context and is used as a title of office after the New Testament church was well under way and growing.

(BAGD): (p. 699) διάκονος A servant of someone; a waiter at a table; a deacon as in an official office within the church. Generally a deacon is a helper who serves in an official capacity. The office likely includes women who meet the qualifications listed.

(M&M): (p.149) διάκονος (1249) There exists abundant evidence to support the application of the word as a description of an office within the Christian church. Ancient history would also support the word as in connection with an office of service to another who is in authority. In B.C. 100 a religious document lists temple officials that include the διάκονος or 'Deacon' operating under the direction of the Priests. There also exist documents linking the 'Deacon' with but separate from the office of 'Priest.' In Romans 16:1 we have the existence of a female serving in the office of Deacon. This idea of an office of Deacon had been prepared in advance for the Christian church by the existence of Deacons who served others in authority in ancient times as in the Church today.

(BROWN): (I. p.544-549) (3) When we speak of serving we imply work done for another, either voluntarily or under compulsion. The activity of serving stands in contrast to ruling; and, serving humbly as opposed to serving with pride. True freedom is found only in the service of God. The word διάκονος has the primary meaning of 'one who waits upon tables.' In Philippians 1:1 and also in 1 Timothy 3:8-13 it is used of a man holding the office of deacon in the church; the same title is given to a woman, Phoebe in Romans 16:1. It may have been the intention of Paul to include women in the office of deacon in 1 Timothy 3:11. Sometimes the New Testament replaces the word 'deacon' with *υπηρεται* (pronounced huperete) which originally meant an under or assistant rower on a ship: Hence, the meaning of a servant helper or attendant who serves to assist someone else who is in authority. The work of deacon eventually developed into a special office which, over time became a standardized form. However, the specific duties are not clearly stated in the NT. Originally, all the work done in the church was referred to as a 'service.' But, in a more specialized sense the office of deacon was narrowed down to the material care of the church and the work is closely linked to the office of Bishop (Overseer). In the ancient Orthodox Church the deacon was retained for service. In the Roman and Episcopalian Churches the deacon became a transitional step on the way to becoming a Priest. The New Testament certainly knows of the existence of a female deacon but her role is left undefined.

(TDNT): (V11, p.88-92) διακονέω In general the word was used to indicate a waiter at a meal, a servant of a master, a servant of a spiritual power, a servant that could also be described as a slave of another, a servant of Christ, a servant of the church. A distinction may be made between all these general uses and the employment of the term as "a fixed designation for the bearer of a specific office" in the developing constitution of the church. In his letter to the Philippians, Paul singles out the people who served in this office of deacon. In order he greeted the Saints, then the Elders and then the Deacons. Important to note that already in this phrase the office of Deacon is here linked with Bishops (Elders) and named after them. At the time of this letter there were two coordinated offices in the church: Overseer and Deacon. We do not have a description of what the Deacon does in the fulfillment of his duties though. Qualifications for serving in the office of Deacon are provided in 1Ti 3:8-13. Like Bishops, they should be blameless and upright, not a liar or given to licentious living and they must rule or manage their household well and be married to only one wife. The primary task of Deacons was in administration and practical service. This can be deduced from the general meaning of the word, from the qualities demanded of them and from their relationship to their Overseers (Elders). Acts chapter 6 may be regarded as indirect evidence of the creation of this office. The earliest sources of information on the office of Deacon link it with the office of Overseer and were never separated from it. The Deacon is not merely the servant of the church, but also the servant of the Overseer. There may be evidence to support the natural use of two offices in the New Testament church from the practice of having two offices in the Jewish Synagogue of the day. The Christian offices of Overseer and Deacon, with the deacon serving at the direction of the Overseer and in support of him seem a natural progression as the church grew. Ancient literature uses the term διάκονος as a servant of Pharaoh; a servant of his Master; of Zeus; of God. In the New Testament the Deacon is the servant of the Church and Overseer falling under the authority of the Overseer. Alongside the Deacons were also the Deaconesses. Their (Biblical) history seems to begin with Rom 16:1 where Paul refers to Phoebe. It is an open question as to whether he refers to her as she occupies a fixed office or simply serves well within the church. Similarly, it is possible that 1Ti 3:11 could be referring to the office of Deacon occupied by a woman, or it could be referring to the wife of a Deacon. We simply cannot be sure, though it is probable that the office of Deacon includes women who meet the character qualifications for the office.

(EOBD): (P.414) There can be found neither grounds nor evidence that would support the existence of women Elders in the church at any time. In the case of deacons, however, there is a good case to be made for the existence of Deaconess. Whether they had the same duties or were put on the same level as male Deacons is unknown. It is clear from Romans 16:1 that Phoebe was in fact a Deaconess as in the office of Deacon. However, this is the only clear instance of a female Deacon in the New Testament. Confirmation can be found in two 2nd century documents that clearly show women occupying the office of Deacon and having the title of Deaconess. These are found in Hermas's Vision (2.4.3) and Similitude (9.26.2). Therefore, it is likely that Phoebe was formally ordained to the office of Deacon in the same way as the original 7 men of Acts Chapter 6.

(VINES): (P.147) διάκονος "Deacon" primarily denotes a servant, either doing servile work or serving as an attendant to someone else. The meaning may be connected to the word which means "to hasten after or pursue" perhaps as a runner. It also refers to the servants of Christ (Elders) who are responsible to share the Good News through the *service or ministry* of teaching and preaching. It became used to describe those who were selected to serve the church in an office (of Deacon). The so-called "seven deacons" of Acts 6 are not mentioned by that name, though the kind of service in which they engaged was of the character of that committed to such. There was one woman deacon listed in the New Testament; Phoebe who is highly regarded by Paul and referred to in Romans 16:1. The term Deacon, when applied to an office is referring to the relationship one has with their work. This is different than a *doulos* or slave which refers more to the relationship one has with their master. Here, in the office of Deacon it is likely that one serves at the behest of a superior, as in an under-rower on a war galley (*huperetes). The superior who functions as manager is the Overseer (Elder).*

Conclusion

It seems likely that the ministry of practical service or helping became an official office within the Christian Church in order to handle the growing tasks needing to be done. Its creation may stem from Acts chapter 6 when the Hellenists complained that their widows were being overlooked in the distribution of food, though we cannot be sure of this claim from the text itself. The overseers (a.k.a. elders) directed the congregation to identify seven men who met certain character qualifications to take the task off the shoulders of the elders in order to free them for their ministry of the Word. Though the word "deacon" was not used, similar words indicating "service" were used. Therefore it is quite possible the church office of deacon was created during this period of growth in church history. Deacons serve the church and the elders. The office exists under the authority of the elders and in cooperation with them. We find strong evidence of a great servant partnership between the offices of elder and deacon. Their duties are not clearly defined, but it is possible to conclude they would be responsible for serving the people in a practical sense. This shift of responsibility removes such work from the shoulders of the elders and thereby helps them fulfill the duty to teach the Word of God and equip believers for ministry. Further, this office seems to include women as qualified to serve. It should be noted from Philippians 1:1 the use of the Greek definite article *τοῖς* (the), which is applied to all the saints, including overseers and deacons (in that order). Here the grammar would strongly suggest both an order and a hierarchy that links these two offices together within the body of Christ. Both offices serve, but oversight is provided by the elders and practical ministry is carried out by the deacons. Meanwhile, all people are equipped for service to everyone in the name of Jesus. Everyone is responsible for evangelism – proclaim the Good News!

APPENDIX B: ANNOTATED BIBLIOGRAPHY

Books Used in the Research for this Work

* The author's favorite and most highly recommended books are noted *

Works used in comprehensive "Word Studies" can be found in Appendix B.

*Adler, Mortimer J. and Doren, Charles Van. *How to Read a Book.* New York: Touchstone, 1972).

It is amazing how often two people can read a passage of Scripture and come up with very different meanings for the words written. Context is king when reading Scripture because a word derives its meaning only within its relationship with other words. The first, and most basic, thing to learn before engaging in a study of the Bible is the knowledge of how to read a book. This work is an excellent place to start.

Anderson, Leith. *Leadership Handbook of Management and Administration: Setting the Vision.* Grand Rapids: Baker, 1994.

Here is a work designed to show the leadership responsibility of the pastor/elder. Emphasis is placed on the need for the elder to set "vision and mission" for the congregation. It provides descriptive evidence of the lack of results achieved by entrenched congregations who do not follow their elders.

Anderson, Robert C. *The Effective Pastor.* Chicago: Moody, 1985.

This book is a handbook for training a new pastor. It covers a variety of topics dealing with the character and responsibilities of a pastor/elder.

It is a helpful guide for preparing a pastor/elder for ministry. As such, it provides valuable information about the position of pastor/elder.

Berkley, James D. *Leadership Handbook of Management and Administration.* Grand Rapids: Baker, 1994.

This book contains a variety of essays and chapters written by a number of ministry leaders as collected and edited by James D. Berkley. The book contains a number of articles that deal with pastoral/elder duties and expectations. It is a helpful handbook to prepare a pastor/elder for ministry.

Bruce, F.F.; Fee, Gordon D.; Stonehouse, Ned B.; General Editors. *The New International Commentary on the New Testament.* Eerdmans: Grand Rapids, 1997.

This is a comprehensive sixteen volume commentary of the New Testament. It is written by a variety of evangelical scholars. Its value to this research is in providing a more precise analysis of Scriptural passages, in context, with respect to the duties and authority of an elder and the development of a special office of practical ministry known as "deacon."

Campbell, R. Alastair. *The Elders: Seniority Within Earliest Christianity.* Edinburgh: T&T Clark, 1994.

This book is an abbreviated form of Dr. Campbell's doctoral thesis on the topic of elders in the early church and the application to the new church of today. Specific value comes from the fact that his view opposes the elder led government in favor of a strict congregational rule. He presents a distinctly Baptist orientation, attempting to prove that no such formal office of elder is called for in Christian churches of today.

*Carnell, Edward John. *Basic Christian Doctrine: The Government of the Church.* New York: Holt, Rinehart and Winston, 1962.

This text is a thorough and Biblically based look at the doctrine of "government in the Christian church." The work deals specifically with the work and authority of the office of elder.

Carson, D.A., Moo, Douglas J., and Morris, Leon. *An Introduction to The New Testament.* Zondervan: Grand Rapids, 1992.

This textbook is a book by book study of the entire New Testament. It discusses issues of authenticity, purpose, critical analysis, and textual meaning. It is valuable as a source of information on the authenticity of the "Pastoral Epistles" as being intended to provide instruction to elders/pastors. It is valuable as a source of insight on the subject of bishops and deacons and the probability that the deaconess had become the norm for women as the New Testament church grew.

*De Koster, Lester and Berghoef, Gerard. *The Elders Handbook: A Practical Guide for Church Leaders.* Grand Rapids: Christian Library Press, 1979.

This is an instruction book designed specifically to help elders develop leadership skills in the church. The format of the book and its instruction is taken primarily from Paul's parting instructions to the church at Ephesus as recorded in Acts 20:28-31. It has value for research because of its well laid out and logical explanation of how an elder can operate as an effective leader according to specific Biblical instruction.

Dockery, David S., Mathews, Kenneth A., and Sloan, Robert B. *Foundations For Biblical Interpretation: A Complete Library of Tools and Resources.* Nashville: Broadman & Holman, 1994.

This is a collection of theological articles written at the seminary level on a variety of topics. Of particular interest to this work is Part III, article #26, *Biblical Theology of The New Testament* by Bruce Corley. In it the author makes a compelling case for the mission and purpose of the church (ekklesia) of Christ.

*Eims, Leroy. *The Lost Art of Disciple Making.* Grand Rapids: Zondervan, 1978.

This book provides insight into what it means to be a disciple and how important it is to have effective and purposeful leadership that teaches believers how to be one. A clear, logical, and well laid out teaching plan is included. It is helpful for this study in its call to be serious at equipping people to serve. Equipping the saints for works of service is the special job of the pastor and teacher (a.k.a. elder). The implication points to servant leadership and cooperation.

Foss, Michael W. *Power Surge.* Fortress Press: Minneapolis, 2000.

This book endeavors to identify six key marks of a good disciple for a changing church. It includes a section on leadership qualifications and training, as well as one on setting vision and mission. It is valuable for this research in presenting a lay person's view of the need for strong leadership for a church to be successful in ministry.

Guthrie, Donald So. *The Pastoral Epistles.* London: Tyndale, 1957.

This book provides detail about the authenticity of the letters from Paul to Timothy and Titus, commonly referred to as the "Pastoral Epistles." Its value is in its analysis of the historical perspective, authenticity, and intent of these letters to be general instructions to people in positions of leadership such as the pastor/elder.

Harrison, P. N. *The Problem of the Pastoral Epistles.* London: Oxford University Press, 1921.

This book offers a discussion of a statistical analysis of the words used in the epistles commonly credited as Pauline. The conclusion is that someone other than Paul wrote the three "Pastoral Epistles." If true, doubt can be cast by pure Congregationalists about the intent of Scripture to place elders in a position of authority. This book presents an opposing view, and not a very convincing one in my opinion.

Henry, Carl F. *Basic Christian Doctrines.* New York: Holt, Rinehart and Winston, 1962.

This book is a collection of theological papers and talks that were written and/or delivered by a variety of well-known theologians. The articles originally appeared in various issues of "Christianity Today" and cover a wide range of topics. One in particular deals directly with the topic of church government in general and specifically the role of elders in that government.

Henry, Matthew. *Matthew Henry Concise Commentary on the Whole Bible.* Quickverse: Electronic STEP Edition CD Rom V7.0, 1998.

This book is a brief commentary designed to aid a person in personal study of Scripture. By itself, it has limited value, but, used in conjunction with other sources and commentaries, it adds value to research because it helps clarify one's understanding of Scripture, particularly in regard to the form and function of elders and deacons.

*Hull, Bill. *The Disciple Making Pastor: Leading Others on the Journey of Faith.* Grand Rapids: Baker, 2007.

This valuable guide will help those who will be elders/pastors achieve their mission to lead people into Christian maturity and equip them for ministry. The book enables one to understand the concepts of servant leadership and clear teaching. In order to understand the role of a pastor, one must understand how to make disciples.

Jamieson, Robert., Fausset, A. R., and Brown, David, *Commentary Practical and Explanatory on the Whole Bible* Zondervan: Grand Rapids, 1962.

This valuable commentary on the whole Bible provides specific assistance to understanding the intent and authenticity of the letters referred to as "The Pastoral Epistles."

Keener, Craig S. *The IVP Bible Background Commentary: New Testament.* Intervarsity Press: Downers Grove, 1993.

This book provides background commentary on every verse in the New Testament with particular emphasis on the cultural understanding of the texts. It is beneficial to this research in identifying what it meant to be an elder at the time of the New Testament in terms of how the people of that day would have understood and accepted it. Also, it sheds some light on the development of the office of deacon that seems to have been created after the New Testament church was well under way.

*Kunjummen, R.D. *New Testament Greek: A Whole Language Approach.* Troy: Emet, 2009.

This is an introduction to the Greek language of the New Testament. An ability to understand the original meaning of words such as elder, overseer, pastor and deacon requires working with the original language. This work is helpful in arriving at a basic knowledge of the Greek language system. It aids in identification of word forms such as verbs, nouns, adjectives, and participles and the impact the form has on the meaning it may have for us today. It is recommended for anyone who would like to become familiar with the basics of Koine Greek.

*LaHay, Tim. *Why You Act The Way You Do.* Carol Stream: Tyndale, 1984.

LeHay provides an excellent description of the various spiritual gifts, talents, and temperament that makes each person who they are and explains why they act the way they do. This is an extremely beneficial aid to team building and in managing people effectively. It can assist a church in helping people identify their unique "shape" for ministry and get them plugged into a team where they can serve Christ with joy and effectiveness. It will help an individual learn more about himself or herself and also how to work better with others.

*MacArthur Jr., John F. *Ashamed of the Gospel.* Wheaton: Crossway, 1993.

This book is a call to return to Biblical teaching. The author is concerned with the trend to water down the Gospel in an attempt to keep from offending people. The focus of the book is on the desperate need for Christians to return to Scripture as the authority and guideline for all decisions. In one section, the author discusses the Biblical role of an elder and provides an excellent outline of Paul's instructions to Timothy as found in 1 and 2 Timothy.

*Mohler Jr., R. Albert. *He is Not Silent: Preaching in a Postmodern World.* Grand Rapids: Moody, 2008.

Mohler supplies a compelling look at the importance of the elder's duty to be serious about serving the "Ministry of the Word of God." The Word is both the source of his authority and the purpose of his office. The postmodern world teaches the idea that we can decide for ourselves what is right or wrong on the basis that "everything is relative." The Word of God stands in stark contrast to the teachings of the world. It simply must become the focus of all Christian ministry.

Olson, Arnold T. *This We Believe.* Free Church Publications, 1961.

This book is an authoritative textbook on the Doctrinal Statement of the Free Church (EFCA). It provides a valuable historical perspective on why the Free Church adopted the Congregational form of government. This particular denomination was involved in the move toward Congregationalism at a very early stage (prior to the Reformation, according to their own scholars).

*Ogden, Greg. *Leadership Handbook of Management and Administration: Servant Leadership.* Grand Rapids: Baker, 1994.

This book provides valuable insight into what it means to be a shepherd of the flock of God. At the heart of the role of shepherd is the idea of "servant leadership." This forms the basis upon which an elder is expected to function.

Osborn, Larry W. *The Unity Factor.* Owls Nest: Vista, 2001.

This book discusses the factors that bring unity to a congregation while equipping them for the work of ministry. Leadership is stressed as a necessary ingredient for healthy church ministry. It is valuable in its explanation of the pastor's role as a leader and in particular the role of "initiating leader."

Packer, James I. *Basic Christian Doctrine: The Nature of the Church.* New York: Rinehart and Winston, 1962.

Packer presents a thorough discussion of how the church of Christ is designed to function. Included in this work are both the topic of elder rule and authority as well as the work of ministry by the congregation.

Richards, Lawrence O. *The Victor Bible Background Commentary.* Quickverse: Electronic STEP Edition CD Rom V7.0, 1998.

This book is a commentary on the entire Bible, with emphasis on background information such as word meanings and cultural items that would impact one's understanding of the text. It is valuable as a resource because it helps to keep one's hermeneutic in proper perspective. That is, it assists in helping one to identify first what a passage meant to the people to whom it was originally written.

*Spangler, Ann and Tverbert, Lois. *Sitting At The Feet of Rabbi Jesus: How the Jewishness of Jesus Can Transform Your Faith.* Grand Rapids: Zondervan, 2009.

This work allows one to come to a clearer understanding of the rabbinic system of teaching that existed in Jesus' day. It is very helpful in coming to grips with the authority of the rabbi and the logical conclusion that this authority now exists in the New Testament church in the office of elder or pastor. To be a disciple who follows the Rabbi, "A Talmidim," means to be a student of the Word of God. The authority of Scripture is paramount, and, in order to learn, one must be taught, which requires a willingness to follow.

*Stowell, Joseph M. *Shepherding The Church: Effective Spiritual Leadership in a Changing Culture.* Chicago: Moody, 1997.

This work is valuable to help one understand the need for strong theology, teaching, and servant leadership. When the mission of Christ is clearly understood, one can see the need for "teaching elders" in the church of Christ. To be effective in the age of postmodernism, leadership that does not water down the Gospel is more important than ever. Along with leadership must come the recognition of authority and a willingness to obey. The mission is clearly divided into three categories: evangelism, identification and discipleship. Effective leadership is needed.

Strauch, Alexander. *Biblical Eldership: An Urgent Call to Restore Biblical Church Leadership.* Littleton: Lewis and Roth, 1986.

This is a well documented and thoroughly researched book on the subject of elders in the church. It is quite valuable for research on the topic of church government. Roles, duties, and qualifications are well explained.

Swindoll, Charles R. *The Master's Plan for the Church.* Insight for Living, 2000.

This booklet, designed as a Bible study companion along with a video curriculum, addresses the Bible's view of church, how it should function, and who should be leading it. The material is quite beneficial to arriving at a clearer Biblical understanding of what God intends the New Testament church to become and how it should be functioning.

Wagner, Peter C. *Leadership Handbook of Management and Administration: Leading Versus Enabling.* Grand Rapids: Baker, 1994.

This work endeavors to expand on one's understanding of leadership within a congregation. It explores the consequences to a church when a congregation does not trust and follow its elder/pastor.

*Warren, Rick. *The Purpose Driven Life.* Grand Rapids: Zondervan, 2002.

This work depicts the plan and purpose that God intended for the life of a believer. This work greatly helps one understand what God created him or her to do. It is a self help book based on the Word of God!

*Warren, Rick. *The Purpose Driven Church.* Grand Rapids: Zondervan, 1995.

This book started my journey of discovering what God expects us to accomplish and how to do it. Through the impact of this book, I developed a stronger desire for discipleship and a passion for discovery that led me to attend seminary. Having fallen under its influence, I was compelled to write my master's thesis on the subject of elders, which has been further developed into my own book. Thank you, Rick Warren.

Watson, J. B. *The Church: A Symposium.* London: Pickering & Inglis, 1949.

This book is a collection of papers written by seventeen scholars, including W.E. Vine and W. R. Lewis, on a variety of topics involving the church and Christianity. The specific paper on "Government and the Church" is particularly helpful for research on the topic of elders and government.

Wiersbe, Warren W. *Wiersbe's Expository Outline of the New Testament.* Colorado Springs: Victor, 1992.

This book is a commentary on the New Testament. It is a chapter by chapter review of the entire New Testament, as each chapter relates to the total revelation God has given about Jesus Christ and His redemptive work. The value for this study is the insight that can be gained from the specific passages where leadership roles are described, both directly and indirectly.

Zuck, Roy B. and Walvoord, John F. *The Bible Knowledge Commentary New Testament Edition.* Wheaton: Victor, 1983.

This book is an exposition on the entire New Testament by the professors and staff of Dallas Theological Seminary. It is a collective effort designed as a brief but reliable commentary on the Scripture. It has a particularly conservative Evangelical perspective and is valuable for additional insight into the meaning of appropriate Scriptural passages for research on the subject of elders, deacons, and church government in general.

CPSIA information can be obtained at www.ICGtesting.com
Printed in the USA
BVOW03s1104050314

346747BV00001B/137/P